1 - ∞

THE COMMONWEALTH AND INTERNATIONAL LIBRARY

Joint Chairmen of the Honorary Editorial Advisory Board

SIR ROBERT ROBINSON, O.M., F.R.S., LONDON

DEAN ATHELSTAN SPILHAUS, MINNESOTA

Publisher: ROBERT MAXWELL, M.C., M.P.

PERGAMON EDUCATIONAL GUIDES

General Editor: F. H. PEDLEY

AWAKENING THE SLOWER MIND

with my love

L. Bruce

978008006386 7

D1744163

AWAKENING THE SLOWER MIND

VIOLET R. BRUCE
M.Ed., Ph.D.

Principal Lecturer in Dance
City of Leicester College of Education

PERGAMON PRESS

OXFORD · LONDON · EDINBURGH · NEW·YORK
TORONTO · SYDNEY · PARIS · BRAUNSCHWEIG

Pergamon Press Ltd., Headington Hill Hall, Oxford
4 & 5 Fitzroy Square, London W.1

Pergamon Press (Scotland) Ltd., 2 & 3 Teviot Place, Edinburgh 1

Pergamon Press Inc., Maxwell House, Fairview Park, Elmsford,
New York 10523

Pergamon of Canada Ltd., 207 Queen's Quay West, Toronto 1

Pergamon Press (Aust.) Pty. Ltd., 19a Boundary Street,
Rushcutters Bay, N.S.W. 2011, Australia

Pergamon Press S.A.R.L., 24 rue des Écoles, Paris 5ᵉ

Vieweg & Sohn GmbH, Burgplatz 1, Braunschweig

First edition 1969

Library of Congress Catalog Card No. 77–80726

Printed in Great Britain by A. Wheaton & Co., Exeter

08 006386 1 (flexicover)
08 006387 x (hard cover)

CONTENTS

FOREWORD

DOCTOR BRUCE is a writer of wide educational experience. She is herself a gifted teacher of children of all ages and abilities; she was for many years an adviser of teachers and, though her professional concern is now with their initial training, she also manages to find time to encourage and help teachers already in service.

She has always been deeply concerned for the welfare of children with difficulties. In the last few years she has visited very many schools dealing with handicapped pupils, and in this book she has set out her observations on them and her conclusions on the way they should be taught.

Those who read her book are likely to be wiser in their understanding of children, to know more about the importance of freeing children from fear, about the dangers of their failure, about the need for excitement, happiness, and exhilaration in the school, and about the learning process at its most effective. In particular, they will appreciate the part that expressive arts can play in stimulating the happy growth and development of children.

But, as is often the case, discoveries about what is best for the slower or handicapped learner illuminates the teaching of more normal children, and her book should help all teachers who read it.

SIR ALEC CLEGG

PREFACE

THIS book concerns children who are in our educational system, the least able of all those whom we classify as educable. They are those children who are offered, and whose parents or guardians accept, places in special schools for the educationally subnormal, those children in special or remedial classes in primary, secondary modern, comprehensive, or high schools, and those who are in the lowest streams or are falling markedly behind others in these schools. I should like to question the description "ineducable" for children who fall short even of the above categories, but this is not the immediate concern of this book.

It is relevant at all times to question contemporary educational methods. Those who have greater success in school than the children I am proposing to discuss do manage to deal in varying degrees of competence with the courses with which our education system faces them. The so-called educationally subnormal child does not. It is certain that for all children there would be enrichment of personal growth if we could enhance the opportunities for their communication, if we could spend a great deal of the time now consumed by memorizing and being tested, in artistic activity, and those experiences which arise from a rich environment. There is often a measure of deprivation for those children who spend their years of adolescence in our grammar schools. Nevertheless, even if one wonders how advantageous a more expressive education would be for these pupils, they are not in the plight of the least able children in our community. They have access to further education and to interesting employment. They are accepted, respected, and self-respecting.

The first part of the study concerns the situation as I saw it and the related problems. Each chapter focuses upon a particular aspect, and there is inevitably the problem of overlapping areas. At risk of repetition and for the sake of clarity, I have written in this way. The second part indicates the ways in which I believe teachers could use the expressive arts and allied activity to help these children to grow in personality and liveliness and to acquire the interest in and need for language which may lead to a lasting literacy for them.

What is said in general applies to children in all schools. A. R. Stone, during the Second World War indicated the educational value of the arts.* Some progress has been made in our schools in this direction, but it is to a large extent and increasingly off-set by competition in educational prowess urged on by parental pressure, and the race among teachers for promotion and status. The most successful children in school are deprived during their childhood of some of the most important riches of life, but the least successful children need help to enable them to take an adequate place in the community and to ensure such a place for their children.

Our infant schools still lead the country in educational progress. They have come to this by understanding the needs of the youngest children. Perhaps the teachers of the children who fail could lead the educational field in the deep and exploring attitudes which they bring to the understanding of the developmental processes for all children with which education must be concerned. Educational services in this country have taken responsibility to a large degree for the upbringing of children, yet very little attention is paid in school to the education of the emotions.

* A. R. Stone, *The Story of a School.*

ACKNOWLEDGEMENTS

I wish to acknowledge my gratitude to the following people:

To all head teachers, members of teaching staffs, administrative and domestic staffs, whose schools I visited in England and Scotland, and in the United States of America, and to all the children who were pupils in these schools.

To those in the factories which I visited who offered their knowledge and experience.

To youth employment officers who answered my letters so thoroughly.

To medical officers who discussed with me, read parts of my script, and answered my questions.

To my typist and friend, Miss Margaret Oates.

To my friend Sir Alec Clegg who has written the Foreword to this book and who has given me constant encouragement.

To Holt, Rinehart & Winston, Inc.; *New Society*, and *The Times* for permission to use material.

LODGED

The rain to the wind said,
"You push and I'll pelt."
They so smote the garden bed
That the flowers actually knelt,
And lay lodged—though not dead.
I know how the flowers felt.

Robert Frost.

PART I

CHAPTER 1

WHO ARE
THE CHILDREN WHO FAIL?

This chapter is intended as a prelude to what follows in this book. It is not written simply as a study of the problems involved and their causes. There are works such as Eleven Thousand Seven Year Olds, *by Dr. Kelmer Pringle, N. R. Butler, and R. Davie;* Cruelty to Children, *by Dr. Chesser;* Heredity and Environment, *by E. G. Conklin; and many others, some of which are listed in the bibliography. These deal much more adequately and authoritatively with the identification of the children who fail in school. This chapter is included, however, because it will be useful for students and teachers who may not have studied some aspects of the problem in depth, and it may lead to further reading and to more detailed knowledge. It provides, moreover, a clear establishment of the areas with which the rest of the book is concerned.*

One aspect stands out clearly as needing clarification for any person who presumes to investigate problems of education for a particular group of children. This is the question, "Who are these children?"

The difficulties facing these children vary very much. Some special schools are the only existing ones for educationally sub-normal children in a county and they draw from a large area. Sometimes children come from neighbouring authorities. Some authorities have both day and residential schools, so that residential places can be reserved for children with severe problems of deprivation, those living far from any special school suitable for them, and those with other handicaps which increase their learning difficulties still further. The degree and nature of the problems contributing to a child's situation vary markedly with the area served by the school. For instance, the deprivation apparent in a large industrial city differs in nature from that of a farming area. There is a difference in the degree and kind of problems encountered in residential and in day schools and further variation in those found in special classes in schools for the "ordinary child".

In order to clarify, I shall discuss these children in areas of handicap which do, of course, overlap. It is necessary to deal with some of the prominent areas more fully. This I have done after establishing the main categories which my observations and inquiries led me to believe existed.

The number of brain-damaged children varies considerably from school to school. There are usually a few children in each residential school with slight hemiplegia or damage involving the function of the limbs. Severely physically handicapped children, seen, few in number, seem nevertheless to fit into the environment quite well. All of these were able to move about the school without a wheel chair or to have ambulatory supports. There are a few microcephalic children. Many more are minimally brain damaged, having difficulties of co-ordination and of learning, and having a history of birth injury, premature birth, phenylketonuria, meningitis, or some pre-natal, peri-natal, or post-natal damage affecting the brain. There are in most schools one or two epileptic children, sometimes four or five. Usually these children are having careful medical attention and are under sedation which keeps their condition in check. Many are only susceptible to minor seizures. Always there seems to be great care taken and the situation is accepted calmly. There appears to be considerable use of sedation to control this and other conditions, and also to help the staff to deal with some of the more severe emotional difficulties.

There is occasionally a child with a severe condition, having a poor prognosis, such as the child with leukaemia or with muscular dystrophy.

Sometimes there are mongoloid children, always high-grade mongols who appeared often to be among the most adjusted children in the group. They have the physical difficulties associated with their disability. Their sight is often poor, they are usually heavily built and sometimes clumsy in movement, although some are very rhythmically sensitive. They are backward in varying degrees, but almost always friendly and happy and on the whole well accepted by the rest in spite of the fact that they looked different.

Always there are children with difficulties of sight and hearing. In most areas very careful investigation is made by post-natal and child welfare clinics and by school medical officers into sight and hearing deficiencies, and in general it is now quite difficult for such a defect to be overlooked for any length of time. Nevertheless, this does still occur with resulting increased learning problems.

In every school there are children with speech defects. There is a strong link between educational subnormality and speech difficulty.

It is a trend of the present day in this country for people to become heavier, and the number of obese children is constantly increasing. In one area, about 2 per cent of the children examined in schools in a particular year were found to be overweight, the sexes being evenly represented. These children were few in the infant schools, but were more in junior schools and there was a sharp rise at the secondary level, there being more obese children in secondary modern schools than in grammar schools. The medical officer reported that 79 per cent of the children who attended the obesity clinic came from lower income groups.* There are many such children among those we are considering. Often they have poor circulations and are lethargic and incoordinate. The most distressing factor is the embarrassment and lack of confidence experienced by these children. The difficulties are accentuated in the senior age groups, more obviously in

* Investigations made by the City of Leicester School Medical Services, 1962–64.

girls' schools, although we may be grossly underestimating the misery and handicap of the obese adolescent boy. For many of these overweight children there is a family history of obesity. Eating habits are no doubt to blame in many cases, but an inherited metabolic factor is often present. Dieting is necessary and obviously there is need to interest teachers, local authorities, meals organizers, and cooks in the factor of carbohydrate limitation and protein provision for these children especially, and for all children in this age of plentiful eating for most people in this country. The problem of obesity is probably treated too lightly by some heads and teachers and by some medical staff.

All schools have a number of children who give evidence of hyperkinetic quality in their movement, speech, and general behaviour. Sometimes there appears to be a majority of children in extreme categories, the lethargic and the over-active.

There are children who have suffered physically through accident or ill treatment, for instance, a child who has had head injuries in a car crash and who has suffered a brain injury, and the tragic case of the father who had caused a child head injury in his violence.

We might wonder how many of the children for whose learning difficulties there seems to be no reason could have been in some way brain-damaged so that they are subnormal in the ordinary school situation.

Many children, especially those who are in residential schools, and especially in senior girls' groups, are severely emotionally disturbed. This could be the cause of their learning difficulty or could be, at least in part, the result of their continued failure. There is, it would seem, most often a combination of cause and consequence—an unhappy, continuing circle.

Many children come from deprived home backgrounds. This is a very extensive and important grouping and receives, among others, further clarification. Another allied and prominent reason for a child being in a special school or department of this kind is the sub-cultural home. A variety of factors contributes to this sub-culture, which differs in rural areas from the crowded street in a large city.

There seems no doubt in the minds of head teachers that the factor of low genetic endowment is a frequent cause of subnormality. Some seemed to consider the factor of inheritance singly and not to relate the environmental-genetic combination which determines the development of a child personally and intellectually. There are many children for whom several factors are probably causing subnormality: as, for instance, the child in a rural school who, over-active, incoordinate, and with major learning difficulties, came from a rural sub-cultural environment, had parents of limited intelligence, and was possibly minimally brain-damaged, there having been evidence of a difficult birth.

Another factor which appears very often is the weak personality of the mother or of both parents. When there is a strong mother, even the worst conditions are less harmful. Often there is evidence of lack of drive and ability to cope with the struggle in life, and often with the strain of a large, young family. Resources are badly managed and sometimes there is promiscuity and inability to make a loyal, functioning home life.

Sometimes there are immigrant children who come from unstable, deprived, or broken homes.

There are children from affluent homes where there is gross mishandling of a child's development, rejection, spoiling, or over protection.

A few are the less able children of intelligent parents with very bright siblings, whose parents are unable to accept a less intelligent child and have made life unbearable for him through pressure and over-expectation.

Sometimes a child has a history of chronic illness and is very backward so that it is difficult to tell whether he could in fact ever learn at a normal level.

Speaking generally, these are the children in the schools who are the failing ones in an educational system, and they are the main kinds of backgrounds of the children with whom we are concerned.

The education of children depends upon their awakening to all the stimuli which surround them. It depends upon the quality and quantity of that which is the child's total environment, the receptiveness of all the senses available, the development of understanding and organization of ideas, and the ability to respond.

This process occurs from the period of intra-uterine growth onwards, and when we are considering the problems for children who are attaining a level of educative behaviour which we term subnormal, we must take into investigation the whole process of development from the beginning of life. When a child enters school the time comes when achievement begins to be measured and selection begins to take place. The part which the child will play in life as an adult does in fact begin to be planned in his early school days. There is a growing awareness of the dangers, the inaccuracies, and inevitabilities of our educational culture, and the climate of thought is ready for honest consideration of the reasons why some children are to be found failing in the normal activities of our schools and are in special classes in our primary and senior schools, in remedial departments, and in schools for educationally subnormal children. So it will be important in this investigation to study the relationship between environment and educational subnormality. How much is there, in fact, for the child to receive?

Education is dependent upon the power of receptiveness, and it is obvious that difficulty in this area, in hearing, in sight, in brain damage, in disability of any kind as well as stress factors which might inhibit receptiveness, must be considered. The level of awareness is dependent upon emotional, mental, and physical activity, and one or more of these areas may be vitally involved.

Learning is dependent upon the ability to understand and to organize ideas which come to consciousness, so that there must be consideration of this area of the problem. What is the reason for confusion here and does the confusion really lie in this process?

Learning is dependent upon the ability to express ideas, to clarify them, and to communicate, in order to share and to express the need for further stimulus. Is it that the child has difficulty in using the language demanded of him? The stammerer finds a problem with speech; many children find word language a difficult one, for many reasons. Quite obviously a physically handicapped or spastic child may find movement and gesture a difficult language. The deaf child is severely handicapped in the process of communication, and gesture is his easiest channel at an early stage. Have we considered sufficiently the interrelationship of the means of human communications?

It will therefore be necessary to investigate fully the area or areas which may be poorly functioning for any child who is in the category of educational subnormality, realizing of course that these areas are interrelated and interdependent.

Damage done in the Environment of the Uterus or at Birth

It must first be said that disorders arising before or at birth are often caused by a combination of environmental and genetic factors. Given a certain environment, certain genetically predisposed babies develop deformities. There is a strong connection between deformity and miscarriage, the majority of malformed foetuses being shed at an early stage. The placenta as the prenatal provider is very important, and much research work goes on in this area of study. We may fully know one day why a baby is born prematurely, and how much oxygen he needs, so that with premature and full-term babies, damage from an excess or deficiency of oxygen may be avoided.

Many deformed babies have only trivial defects and many of these can be corrected to apparent normality by early treatment. Handicaps, slight or major as they may be, can occur as a result of faulty pre-natal environment, but they affect in varying degrees the other areas concerned in the learning process which we are discussing.

The sensory area may be involved, as when a child is born without sight; the organization, regulation, and retention of material may be rendered poorly functioning as when there is damage affecting the area of brain responsible; or communication may be impaired as in the "thalidomide" child whose limbs may be vestigial.

Often damage is not readily recognized, so that when considering children who for some reason do not succeed in general education at a reasonably normal level, the possibility of damage at or before birth must be entertained.*

There are in all schools for educationally subnormal children and in most special classes children who are in some way handicapped because of pre-natal or peri-natal damage or disturbance of normal development. Schools vary tremendously in the number of such children in their care, residential schools having the largest number.

My observations led me to believe that some children who were not in this category in the minds of teachers in the schools, should have been there, and that for many children there existed a factor of such handicap which was unrevealed and knowledge of which would at least have helped the teacher to understand a child more fully.

> The critical period in the formation of any single structure or function of the body is brief. It may last only a few hours or a few days, and even in the case of the most elaborate systems, not more than two or three weeks.†

Some children with whom we are concerned have suffered damage during the first trimester of pregnancy when the major organs and tissues are being formed.

The whole of the mother's previous life, her health, her own physical endowment, her nutrition before and during pregnancy is important. A mother's vitamin deficiency can cause abnormality in a child. There is then a social, economic, and educational

* Dossiers are being compiled on 13,500 Newcastle upon Tyne children. The survey was begun in 1960 by the Department of Child Health in the Royal Victoria Infirmary, Newcastle. Its aim is to establish the earliest indications and causes of various handicaps in later life (*Yorkshire Post*, March 1966).

† M. Ashley, *Life before Birth*, p. 12.

link here. A factor in the perpetuation of subnormality becomes obvious.

There is a definite relationship between the health of a mother and the chances that a child may be still-born or born prematurely, or of the birth being a difficult one. If a mother has poor health the baby, even if he is born normal, may start life with susceptibility to early illnesses such as colds, bronchitis, or rickets, and so he is deprived of a normal chance of educational success. The tiredness and worry which many mothers suffer during pregnancy cannot be discounted when one considers the chances a child has of developing healthily and normally. "A long time study in Aberdeen, Scotland, covering 17 years, showed the same correlation; deficient nutrition in the mother was closely related to malformation in the child."*

The danger to the child from infections suffered by the mother must be mentioned here. German measles in early pregnancy is responsible for abnormalities in a child. This factor is clearly established. Poliomyelitis brings great dangers to the life of the foetus. Syphilis is especially damaging unless appropriate treatment is given in time.

The whole question of the supply of oxygen to the unborn child is under continuous study. This is most certainly a crucial matter when one considers the number of children in special schools for whom lack of oxygen before or at the time of birth may well have been a factor in the determination of the failure to develop normally. Anaesthetics, sedatives, and drugs taken by the mother, even smoking, can reduce the supply of oxygen to the unborn baby. The premature child is not ready to rely wholly upon his own breathing capacity. The lengthening of uterine contractions by drug administration can interfere with the baby's supply of oxygen.

> There is evidence that even mild anoxia may cause some slight damage to the brain. Some reading difficulties for example are now believed to have their source in brief periods of oxygen starvation before and during birth. And some behaviour problems may be traceable to the same origin.

* *Ibid.*, p. 31.

... How can we say that a child might have been brighter if he had had more oxygen in his blood stream? We cannot: but there is the possibility.*

One sees in schools children with speech disorders, reading disability, behaviour problems, children who are hyper-kinetic and whose powers of concentration are inadequate for schooling as we present it to them. Such disorders all make one concerned about possible causes in pre-natal and in peri-natal life. Are these preventable?

In schools for educationally subnormal children and in special classes one usually finds a few epileptic children. Some of them may also result from brain damage due to lack of oxygen at birth, particularly in the premature baby.

There is the factor of the biological age of the mother. The children concerned are sometimes the offspring of very young mothers, perhaps unmarried mothers who may have little care in pregnancy and for whom this has probably been a time of great emotional turmoil. There is evidence, too, that the woman who is over 35 may have a greater chance of giving birth to a mongol child or to a child with some form of mental handicap.

The matter of drugs and the pregnant woman came dramatically to light when "thalidomide" children were born. Quite obviously there is danger that drugs prescribed for the mother's body may cross the placental barrier and cause harm to the child. Antibiotics, whilst possibly protecting in some situations, may also be harmful.

A mother may affect her baby because she suffers from a defective thyroid gland or from diabetes. She may be merely pre-diabetic. She may be anaemic. These conditions are treatable and there is no need for this baby to be harmed. One can only emphasize the importance of medical care for the pregnant woman. Subnormal children from deprived homes have so often deprived mothers, and the result for the child is multiple handicap.

Brain damage might result from allergies and blood incompatibilities, such as the Rhesus factor incompatibility. This area is not fully understood, but there is possible cause here.

* *Ibid.*, p. 45.

One must consider the great importance of emotional disturbances, stress, and fatigue, and the relationship between the mother's emotional state and the stability, adequate nourishment, and healthy development of the baby.

Finally, the act of birth itself might be responsible for damage to the child. If the birth is a difficult one, damage might be inflicted even by the help brought by the doctor. If there is delay, the oxygen supply could be interrupted sufficiently to cause damage.

I have dealt with this topic in some detail because I have been increasingly disturbed by the number of children who seemed to have possible damage and by the lack of awareness of some teachers of this possibility. Not only would more knowledge help us to find the channels through which we might reach these children in communication, but it would surely help us to assess and understand the child's difficulties. One hopes, too, that the task of prevention might be reinforced, and that the socio-economic factor bringing about many dangers to the unborn child might be adequately faced. "Thus the elimination of poverty could result not only in fewer defective births, but also prevent the exacerbation of existing defects."*

The Environment after Birth

When a baby is born his effector mechanism is more prepared for life than his affectors. Those activities which are already functioning are those important for survival and are largely automatic. A very young baby can grip, open his mouth and suck, given the necessary stimuli. There is a rhythm of sleeping and waking which the outside world later transforms into a diurnal variation. If one considers the premature and the normally born baby, both babies will walk at approximately the same developmental time, and other innate activities occur near to the time laid down in development. Some activities are, however, dependent upon the child's outside environment. Babies all make

* H. Wortis and A. Freedman, Poverty before and after premature birth, *New Society*, September 1965.

burbling noises; hearing children go on to develop more organized noise until they use speech, but deaf children may lose even their burbling. Listening is necessary to the development of speech in the normal way.

Myelination of the tracts of the brain, thought to be closely related to brain development, and especially to further development of the cerebral cortex, seems to depend upon the child's being subjected to the stimuli of the outside environment. A bird's song is innate, but it is only by hearing other birds that grace notes are learned. A child's development at this early stage is also dependent upon his being in an environment. To understand the response of a child to educative processes and instead of making premature judgements about his ability, one must as far as is possible investigate the nature and quality of his world from earliest years.

Home and parents constitute the world of a very young child, that which goes on in spite of everything, where reassurance is, where a physical form of loving, cuddling, fondling, a gentle voice, feeding, and comforting exist. Mother survives and meets needs. Spreading out into a wider, colder, dangerous world is made possible because she is there. Many children do without this secure beginning, many have only a partial share. Children who are so deprived may survive and grow with fair ease into the outside world, but beginning deprivation is vitally contributory to the possibility of later difficulty.

The birth of another baby is always a blow to the security of a child and can be disturbing even with the utmost care and understanding. Separation from mother can occur in this and in many other ways and may be a disturbance more severe than is obvious at the time. In the present day a young family may well be living away from relatives, and the need of a temporarily motherless child is not served so readily as it could be when grandmother, sisters, and aunts lived in the immediate neighbourhood as in villages and working-class districts of large towns. The mothering of a baby is vitally important to early adjustment. It is personal, alive, and physical, the physical things representing love. A baby may suffer from lack of security in this sense wherever difficulties and stresses arise in the home, as they are so easily communicated to the child, needing as he does to be so often in his mother's arms. Adopted babies are liable to suffer if there is stress existing within the set-up of the adopting marriage or home or within the adopting mother. The system of baby fostering is liable for investigation, there being grave doubt as to the satisfaction of conditions in homes where a woman may take many children primarily for monetary gain.

Let us look at the environment which a good home provides for the young child: there is comfort and healthy living, warmth, cleanliness, and provision for bodily needs. There is some degree of order in surroundings, and some measure of the good things of everyday life, mealtimes, a table laid pleasingly, cosiness of bath and bed time, extra care at times of sickness. There is security, some measure of regularity, guidance, and discipline. There is conversation, colour, and interest in the form of pictures, ornaments, wallpaper, decoration, and photographs. Maybe there is music, almost certainly television, radio, and sounds of all kinds. Perhaps there are other children in the family, a dog, or cat. Mother or father may tell stories or sing songs at bed time. They may make sure that television and radio programmes specially designed for children are put on and may even share them with the children. Saturdays and Sundays are different and there are highlights, shopping, outings to the park, to the circus or pantomime, or to friends or relatives. Holidays mean travelling, the seaside, new places, and new people. There may be a garden and special place for play, a swing or a sandpit, maybe even just a dirt patch. In all there will be interesting and interested parents who can be gentle and also firm and definite, but who also might be sometimes bad tempered and cross, rough, or clumsy.

Within this or a reasonable share of this level of environment a child will stand a good chance of being secure and of being stimulated by the excitement and wonder of living. We know that the greatest need of children beyond that of sheer survival is that of "belonging", which might receive the description "love".

Repeatedly in education one is surprised at the way in which children and students overcome very difficult, inadequate, or crude backgrounds. The outside world, neighbourhood, school, and other persons outside the home have influence. Early home deprivation has without doubt much influence upon the future mental health of a child. This is of concern in this book because mental health is closely associated with learning ability. The importance of environment to the child in the learning situation must be considered where we are concerned with educational subnormality, where environmental starvation may be an important factor.

This brings us to the environment which might very easily supplement and counterbalance the effect of an inadequate home at this early stage—the nursery school. The child whose mother goes out to work and who is left daily at a nursery school or in a nursery class in an infant school may suffer a traumatic experience in the parting from mother and home at an early age for a strange, wider environment. However rich these surroundings may be in stimuli and care, one has always to consider the early break from mother–child relationship, the possible stress of hurry, bustle, and anxiety involved in getting off in the morning, and perhaps the rather abrupt and short-tempered handing over of a child of 2 or 3 years to a nursery teacher in a relatively large, noisy place, where the one-to-one relationship cannot be.

Nevertheless, nursery schools and classes are usually places where there are kind people, where there are colour and materials, space, and other children. Here a child learns at an early stage to share. He has companionship, speech, and human noise going on around him. Routine, habit formation, and physical care are established. The environment is rich with play opportunities and stimulation. For the child whose mother is working, or who would otherwise be deprived of the companionship of other children until school age, or for the child in an apartment home with very restricted space, a nursery school is a necessity.

Unfortunately it is not easy to measure deprivation and to make sure that children whose early environment is poverty stricken in any way have the opportunity of nursery school places. Neither can one take out of the hands of parents who obviously are not aware of or not caring about their child's deprivation of environment, the early upbringing of their family.

In any case, at the time of writing, there is a place in a nursery school for fewer than four children in one hundred, and money and teachers are necessary to provide nursery education for those children for whom it may well mean the ability to benefit from education in the normal school rather than the need for special education.*

Much has been written about the place of play in the whole development of the human being. It is vital that the whole area of play opportunity is included when considering the environment of a young child. A child will play with its own body, but surroundings, materials, and companionship and good teaching all stimulate the natural urge to play. Most children, even given the minimum of opportunity, will play. Where this does not happen there is a deep emotional problem. Through play, problems are solved; a child begins to master anxiety; he gains experiences, explodes aggression, and derives much pleasure.

It is relevant here to mention the tremendous importance to a child that he is from the beginning of life in the outside world in an environment where speech is taking place. The need to compensate the deaf child for lack of speech contact is urgent at a very young age, and other children can be markedly deprived if for some reason they are not in contact generously with speech. The whole problem of child deprivation and its relationship to subnormality must be considered, and here the existence of an environment where the spoken word is abundant and the importance of the quality of language are prominent factors.

Recent research work carried out by the sociological research unit of the University of London Institute of Education (1966) emphasizes the way in which the attitudes of parents concerning

* Figures quoted in *New Society*, March 1967.

the support and preparation of children beginning school, favours markedly those from more privileged homes. Some parents find out about the school, talk to their children about their new venture, and take them along. Many children have no such support or interest. They have parents who do not consider such care their "job", and these on the whole are parents who themselves have little interest in books, whose understanding of the value of toys for their children is limited, and for whom "play" is not part of education. We are fortunate in this country in that we have in our infant schools clearness of vision, child-centred concepts, stabilized now by establishment. Infant education in England has through many years become progressively enlightened in its aims and values; and experience has to a great extent clarified and modified where necessary progressive ideas which were in danger of being used without sufficient thought of the situation or of the understanding of purpose. Our infant schools, in spite of large classes, are very largely places of real education where children are active, working without censure, as near to their own rate as a teacher is able, and are living daily in a school environment which is full of colour, interest, and activity.

It is, of course, still true that there are schools and classes in schools where a child could lack attention and stimulus, where a teacher either does not notice or does not care sufficiently about a child who comes to a school dirty, untidy, or late, or who lags behind in liveliness and apparent ability.

It would be true to say, however, that the environment of most of our infant schools is approaching that which is rich and stimulating for any child and that an infant boy or girl who appeared to be subnormal would usually be better catered for in the infant school whilst of infant age than in a school for educationally subnormal children if his presence was not grossly disturbing to the teacher or other children.

One is often impressed by the place found by the less-able child or even the severely handicapped child in a village classroom. In such schools an epileptic, spastic, or otherwise handicapped child often develops remarkably well, as does the less able child, helped by the other children, belonging very distinctly to the group, and suffering a minimum of disturbance because of his inability to join in some normal activities. I remember the spastic girl who had her legs in irons who was so important to the dance class because she played the percussion. This situation, where children accept the less-able one, take care of him, help in his difficulties, and stimulate his efforts by their own achievements, is an ideal one which cannot always come about, but it is a situation which in many of our infant schools can easily exist.

The environment of a child in the primary school is an increasingly widening one, where school and neighbourhood are able more and more to augment that of the home. Security, love, care, and the stimulus of a lively home environment are still very important. The neighbourhood, contemporaries, and the freedom to enter the wider world become necessary to personality development and learning capacity. The liveliness of the street or the village community of children, the surroundings of town, or the activity of the countryside, can be a balancing influence where learning stimuli are concerned, to the impoverished home background. Compare for one moment the attitude of the parents who rate highly the need for their children to learn, to pass tests and examinations, instil tension in the children and to some extent influence the attitude of schools towards measured and measurable learning, with the parent who wrote:

Dear . . . ,
   pleas Dont let the childre bring henny Moor book home at all they come to school to read Book and not at home if they come with henny Moor book i shall burn them thank you.

Mrs. . . .*

In the first instance the parents may cause gross disturbance for their child, but it is likely that the house has books and that the child has toys and equipment to encourage the learning processes according to the ideas of the parents, however misguided their motives.

* "No comment", *The Times Education Supplement*, November 1964.

It is difficult to imagine how a child in a home, mothered by the writer of the above letter, could avoid disturbance and frustration, and how such an attitude could do anything but hinder even a child's urge to learn.

The environment of the junior school has in many instances, and especially in some areas, followed the tendencies of the infant school in activity, the exploratory nature of children's work, child centredness of teaching, and care for the individual. The bridge between infant and junior school is, however, still often a severe one for children to cross. One still sees in junior schools children in rows of desks, in bare-looking classrooms, heads deep in books or paper, or eyes lifted or wandering whilst teacher "teaches". Often the hall is empty and the morning being "three R's time", the school is still. For this condition the 11-plus examination has in all likelihood been held to blame. There are in England very many lively primary schools where the work is exploratory and creative and children search knowledge in rich surroundings. In such schools artistic work is important and plays a large part in school life. As long ago as the war years A. R. Stone was head of such a school, and many have proved for themselves that interest, creativity, and freedom from classroom and subject imprisonment do not mean less success even in an 11-plus test situation. Since the war, movement towards the rich, active environment where integration, group activity, freedom of choice, and toleration of individual needs has advanced; but competition, pressure from parents, and the academic pattern of our senior and higher education have promoted the school based upon schemes which are believed to be the best guarantors of academic results for the more obviously able pupils.

There are many factors which may contribute to a child's failure in our system of education and to try to be precise and to sort the children into categories would be futile. The causes of subnormality which appear to lie in the environment are many, complicated, and interlocked.

We recognize as never before in this country the inequalities in educational opportunities for our children. We know, however, that there is a proportion of children who are deprived of normal opportunity because of the circumstances of their birth, apart from the measure of their equipment to deal with life.

The health of the educationally subnormal child is in general much poorer than that of the child in the ordinary school. Percentages quoted in *Educational Psychology* (vol. 34, part 3), were that 54·4 per cent of children examined in schools for educational subnormal were in general good health against 87·6 per cent of normal children. This relates to poor environment and living standards.*

There is a greater tendency for the subnormal child to be of low vitality, to have sores, boils, spots, and rough skin (often signs of poor health and malnutrition). These children, for physical and psychological reasons, often have poor posture; they tend to be pale and sometimes underweight.

The health factor may contribute largely to a child's inability to concentrate. Often the home is a crowded one, sleeping accommodation is inadequate, and there is lack of fresh air. Mothers tend to be ignorant about food values and the diet is lacking in the more expensive proteins and fats, in mineral and vitamin content. Such mothers believe in "old wives' tales", and proper medical attention is not always obtained when necessary. There is an increasing tendency for the children to become addicts to pill taking, as when a remedial-class child brings aspirins to school just in case she should not feel well later, and another takes a seasick pill to prepare for her travel to the swimming baths in the town! These children, pulled down in the ordinary school by sheer ill health, often quickly become lively, active, and healthy in a residential school, and one is faced with the socio-economic problem of subnormality, fearing regression for the child if he returns home and to normal schooling.

The Newsom Committee found that there was definitely a

* America's war on poverty has revealed that undetected health problems of the enrollees in the youth corps (neighbourhood centres to help school drop-outs and the "disadvantaged") may be as high as 60 per cent (*New Society*, November 1966).

tendency for less able pupils to be smaller and slighter than brighter ones. They are more likely to be away from school for constant small illnesses or because of illness in the household.

This is perhaps surprising when one considers the advances made in the general physical condition of school children over the past 50 years. In 1944 the duty to provide treatment was extended to all forms of medical care for all children at maintained schools. The 1944 Act made it obligatory for local education authorities to provide school meals and milk, and there has been intelligent and increasingly good provision for physical education in schools for many years. Children in general are taller and heavier, and rickets and other diseases of malnutrition have largely disappeared. The Chief Medical Officer's Report, *The Health of the School Child*, 1962 and 1963, H.M.S.O., states:

> In the social circumstances prevailing in Britain today it is difficult to justify school doctors giving so much of their time to the examination of such a large number of healthy children, when so many other children with serious handicaps, personal problems, emotional or educational difficulties, need much attention and study.

It is possible that the health factor, even associated as it is with lack of parental care and intelligence, overcrowding, and disordered living, should soon become one of the lesser problems which beset the children in our schools for the educationally subnormal. Bad housing, lack of attention, and lack of the intelligence to use money well are, however, important factors contributing to the ill health of children. There is still in this country the possibility of chronic ill health and consequent frequent absence from school being a contributory cause of educational subnormality.

For a large number of the children in these schools and special departments, the place he or she calls home hardly merits such a name. It is probably crowded and dirty, lacking in order or peace. Nights are noisy and wakeful, furniture broken and sparse. There is no privacy, no colour, no loveliness. There may be dirt, vermin, and squalor. Distressing as this may be, it would not be so harmful if it were also a place of security, acceptance, and love. I wondered, when I talked with teachers, they expressing the horror of the kind of home conditions from which the children came of dirt and chaos, if this was as important as some of them thought. Some schools in the ugliest areas of the West Riding of Yorkshire are bright and attractive inside, in striking contrast to the streets outside and probably to the homes from which the children come. Loveliness, colour, and richness of environment are important; cleanliness, order, and restfulness are important; but most important is the human relationship, and it is here that the most severe harm and inhibition to learning is produced. Children who live in this sub-cultural background have great disadvantages and stand a chance of being subnormal in a school-learning situation, but many with adequate resilience and good teaching have overcome these provided that they have had a home which gave some measure of acceptance and security.

It is relevant to mention here the situation in some areas where council houses are concerned. There is, without doubt, hostility in some places and fear in many of the council estate. Such an estate means to the private owner, however humble his own means, dirt, noise, rows, many children, thriftlessness, no pride, bad language, litter, and possibly "jail birds". Here are the "riff-raff" of humanity. Council estates vary, of course, having their reputations even with firms offering hire purchase. There is often a slum-clearance stigma. A school which draws its community wholly from such an estate often has the possibility of behaviour problems and a larger number of children with learning difficulties than a school with a mixed intake.

Too often these homes have a characteristic "greyness". "I went to one house where there were two TV sets, one in each of the downstairs rooms. The woman had her baby delivered on a pile of old army coats. The garden sprouted bottles."*

Even estates seem to be graded so that the "better" families live together on the "better" estates, and the least socially accept-able in older or less well-appointed building ventures. The "least

* H. Land, Provision for large families, *New Society*, November 1966.

suitable" applicants often do not even qualify for a house and so they remain in the oldest dwellings near the centre of cities.

Many children who do not succeed in school come from the less socially acceptable housing estate, characterized by the sameness and drabness of the houses, or from the old slums. Some of our educationally subnormal children come from homes where there are large, unplanned families, illegitimate children, frequent quarrelling between father and mother, promiscuity, and drunkenness. There is only a brief duration of mother–baby relationship because there are frequent pregnancies; feeding habits are haphazard; mother may go out to work when possible and children play in the street from an early age. Justice is rough and the children take hard knocks both inside and outside the home.

There is the whole problem of belonging. There may be no father or no lasting relationship between mother and father. The child may be constantly moved from relative to relative, there being no real stability. It may be that the home is an institution where steady, healthy, and kindly as it may be, there is a lack of individual love and a constant need for regimentation which is not home-like.

Sometimes a child suffers from relationship with a mother who has emotional problems which are excessive, an unmarried mother, or one who has herself been brought up in an institution or foster home and has suffered disturbance as a result. Sometimes fostering, which is of short-term duration, can be an extremely unstable factor in the life of a child.

One of the main groups living in poverty in Great Britain even today are those families with many dependent children—five, six, seven, eight, or more. Sometimes there is also chronic illness of mother or father. Often basic wages are low and a mother with so many children cannot go out to work even between pregnancies. There is a strong likelihood that such a family will be living in less than adequate physical conditions. There are many subsidies which such a family can receive—free school meals, free welfare foods, perhaps council accommodation; but there are many reasons why these are not used—reasons of ignorance, pride, or negligence. Where a social worker is in touch with a family such help may be more readily available, but it is evident that help is necessary for families who need it without the fear that they will be labelled "poor".

A parent may be dull, apathetic, psychopathic, or suffering from chronic or mental illness. Children, especially girls, may be inadequately clad. Money is spent as soon as it is gained on cigarettes, luxuries, anything, because money "burns a hole in the pocket". There is no plan in the home. The washing lies about in piles, and beds are unmade; family meals, the neatly laid table, family outings, and holidays, do not exist.

There is little training. Discipline is maintained through haphazard violence, demands made upon the children being conflicting and unpredictable. There is not economic deprivation so much as lack of sympathy and understanding in human relationship and lack of rhythm in life. Such parents and children develop a resentment of authority, "a chip on the shoulder". Education is treated with little respect, and a child is kept away from school to mind the baby or to do the washing. There is hatred of the police and sometimes hatred of Dad. I quote from a child's essay about her dream world: "We will have a garden and a living room and my Dad will not be there."

These children may see destruction and violence in their homes, often committed in drunken temper. They, too, spend their energy and bored moments in aimless destructiveness, breaking bottles, and destroying plants and trees.

To them sex is a dirty thing. It is a pleasure for the man which the woman "puts up with" and avoids whenever possible. The girls, having obtained very casual knowledge, grow up often to connect sexuality with shame and with exaggerated modesty.

A head teacher spoke to me of the numbers of fathers of her children who were in prison and of the mother who said "and the longer they keep him there the better". Another head teacher spoke of the lack of ability of some of the mothers of his children to manage their homes. There were piles of washing on chairs, piles of dirty clothes in corners, and children had not clothes ready for them to come to school and were therefore often absent. It is difficult for a child from such a background to alter his standards. There is often a conflict between school and home because one must not act "differently" or be a "show off".

Children treated harshly, even brutally, or neglected, may be so because of the foolishness, sickness, or sheer distraction of a mother who cannot cope with the difficulties in her life. Parents may be repressive or extremely harsh, and a child may be beset with fear which inhibits vigorously the ability to learn and normal personality development. Parents may be lacking in affection, cold and detached, or they may be over-indulgent or inconsistent. A mother and father who lack unity may find an outlet for their disharmony in the treatment of the children.

Such factors predispose marked behaviour problems in children as surely as they predispose difficulties in learning and in personality development, the effect of the deprivation in all factors depending upon the ability of a child to adjust and to use his neighbourhood and school to compensate for his circumstances.

There is striking association between disturbance of behaviour and lack of maternal affection in many cases, and a strong association between behaviour problems and learning difficulty. The deprivation of maternal love in particular at an early age is one of the most important factors controlling the mental well-being of a child.

Occasionally I came across a child in a residential school whom I was told had been seriously physically injured by a parent. Typical of these few was a child called "Face" by a teacher who meant it good naturedly. She had had a broken nose and had been brutally handled by her father.

The N.S.P.C.C. still deals with cases of cruelty. Often these cases are difficult to prove. *New Society*, 17 June 1965, reports one inspector who in a suburban area had had nine cases of cruelty in the previous year, in all of which he had obtained convictions. As he said, however, taking cases to court may be undesirable "because you spoilt any work you might do afterwards". The Society does not find it easy to keep in touch with a family when it has successfully prosecuted a parent. Most cases come to the attention of the N.S.P.C.C., however, because of neglect or inadequacy rather than actual brutality.

I quote from this article which describes a family situation typical of that from which some children in E.S.N. schools come, one not of intentional deprivation or cruelty but of inadequate parents of low mentality and resources, unable to do better without help.

I visited one neglect case that must be typical. It involved a family of five who had been evicted from a Council house, then temporarily rehoused in a property due for demolition. When I arrived with the inspector the oldest son, who was 15 and looked 12, was lying on a filthy sofa, covered by a torn blanket. He is supposed to be going to a boarding school for the educationally subnormal but arrangements are held up. A younger son is also to go. The father said he would get a job as soon as the boys went away. The room the family congregated in was dirty, and so were the children. But it was easy to believe the inspector when he said that they were an affectionate unit and that the father was truly concerned about his children's welfare. The children had a dog and one of the boys nursed a kitten as he crouched in a cupboard behind a decrepit armchair. The Family Service Unit was also interested in the family and had been worried about the father, being anti-authority, would react badly to the uniformed N.S.P.C.C. officer. But the father seemed friendly enough and grateful for the officer's help about the schools.

In another case I saw, housing was the crucial problem of a family of eleven children living in a basement. The wiring had been condemned so there was no electricity. The kitchen was built under the stairs, in what might have been a coal hole, which ought to have been condemned. The mother was in bed but quite talkative and cogent. She mentioned some discarded baby clothes she was going to wash and give the inspector. Her husband was pottering about with an enormous boil on his chin, dealing with the children. He said he had just lost his job because the electrician whose mate he had been, had been laid off. He said that he would go to the Labour Exchange the following day. The children ranged themselves on sofa and floor, as though posing for a family album. There was no suggestion of any cruelty. The children were pale and quiet, perhaps too quiet, but it would be difficult to let eleven children run wild in two rooms. They were all very clean, and they were not allowed to play in the yard in case they trampled mud into the room. The inspector promised to go to the Town Hall again to see about new accommodation for them.

Many of the children in E.S.N. schools come from backgrounds such as these described, where the deprivation results from weakness, immaturity, lack of drive, energy, and persistence on the part of parents. They are often easy going, easily led, friendly, and gullible. They may be withdrawn and solitary. Some lie and cheat without conscience, their thinking is rigid, they appear to be selfish and demanding, illogical in their approach to situations and people.

For these parents life is very difficult. The environment changes in pattern, amenities, regulations, work, and leisure; everything changes and they cannot make these adjustments. They are frustrated and insecure. A mother cannot cope with her growing family, but she cannot bring herself to visit a birth-control clinic. Her husband may be in prison and life is altogether too much for her. Her behaviour is emotionally immature and unstable.

The children of such parents tend to have the same outlook and lack of ability to deal with changing situations. Theirs, too, is so often a lack of persistence and drive, and this, combined with inadequacy of home provision and encouragement, makes school a very unpleasant place. These children can be bewildered by school and are quite unable to cope with its demands. They become apathetic and listless rather than troublesome, sitting dull-eyed and unaware, and making only shallow relationships. There is poor ability to strive and truly subnormal personality development, dynamically inferior. "Weakness is the gravest single defect in any inadequate personality. . . . the really weak are doomed!"*

There is often in association with educational subnormality emotional instability and over-lability expressing itself through rapid temperamental changes and explosions of rage.

The factor of immaturity is one which is encountered in many children in schools for the educationally subnormal. It is not by any means only found in children from weak and deprived backgrounds. Indeed, there is possibly a factor in some cases of over-indulgence in an affluent home. In junior special schools one

* C. J. C. Earl, *Subnormal Personalities*, p. 85.

sees charming, friendly children who could not cope with the roughness and toughness of the large primary class.

These children are particularly vulnerable where sexual offences are concerned. They are friendly to strangers, often craving affection and physical contact.

> Perhaps the most significant single characteristic of sexually assaulted children is their tendency to seek affection. . . . Basically, all children who had been assaulted possessed a considerable need for affection, but the E.S.N. children were less repressed in its expression. This fact may help to explain the unexpectedly high proportion of E.S.N. children found in this group and in other groups of sexually assaulted children studied. One may suppose that as a group E.S.N. children experience greater difficulty than other children in responding appropriately to the extremely confusing mores of society. Where their personality needs are in conflict with societal prohibitions they may also find greater difficulty in controlling themselves.*

With older girls, too, the problem is serious. They are often physically mature at 12 or 13, are very vulnerable to flattery, gifts, and affection. Sexual delinquency is only another symptom of inadequacy and of their need for love, care, affection, and success.

The disturbance factor in cases where a parent has committed suicide is worthy of mention here. Such a child can be guilt-laden, withdrawn, distrustful, or aggressive, lacking the relief of communication because there is a hushing up in the family of this "shame". Such children inevitably find school a difficult place and learning a task impossible for them to deal with adequately.

One finds children who are suffering from the continual and severe hurt of rejection, adopted children who have not been truly taken into a home with love, a child of a broken home, or an illegitimate child where there is no true belonging. There was the child who had a half-sister in the same school. Her sister was visited by their mother whilst she was ignored. Children feel rejected for many reasons. They may be of the wrong sex for parental pleasure; more often they are not successful or attractive enough and are rejected in favour of more successful siblings. Children can be rejected because of the sheer inadequacy of

* L. Burton, The assaulted child, *New Society*, May 1965.

parents who may be in prison, engaged in prostitution, or living with another man or woman, and are uncaring about the child. Rejection is one of the strongest and most inhibiting factors in the emotional development of children, and it is a very difficult task to overcome this sufficiently for a child to take a responsible and active part in the process of his normal development. Later I will discuss the part which even school itself may play in the rejection of children.

Head teachers of schools for the educationally subnormal appear in conversation to accept very readily the idea that many children are backward because they are not endowed with intelligence. There are those who, as Kenneth Mather puts it:

> Are the end of the tail of continuous distribution among normals and may be confused with others whose mental deficiency springs from single gene differences as in phenyl-ketonuria.*

Later in this book he states:

> Generally however where the dwarf or the dull is the extreme expression of the continuous variation among normals, his parents and his siblings will be rather short or rather dull, whereas those whose abnormality traces to single gene differences will appear in families most of whose other members give no indication of any special tendency towards shortness or dullness.†

There is in the case of most of the so-called educationally subnormal who have no disturbance of physical make-up, a combination of inheritance with environment which is difficult or impossible to disentangle. There is interplay of genotype and family environment. Where learning takes place at a very early age its effects resemble those of genes. This works surely in reverse. There can be a low level of social development reflecting the failure of a whole population to use fully a perfectly adequate genetic capacity as we see in some tribal communities.

It is extremely difficult to come to any conclusions about the measurement of learning ability or intelligence level and we cannot measure the possibilities of attainment for children who

* K. Mather, *Human Diversity*, Introduction.
† *Ibid.*, p. 73.

have what seems to be poor intelligence endowment. It has been stated:

> Observations on twins and foster children would seem to indicate that the variation in I.Q. is about three-quarters due to gene differences, and one-quarter to other causes. Certainly it is highly unlikely that the genes are responsible for anything less than half the variation in I.Q. of our population.*

Many of the children in both day and residential schools for the educationally subnormal have a low apparent genetic endowment of learning capacity and a very deprived social background. This is an obvious and likely combination.

The Immigrant Child

In day schools there arises at this time the problem of learning for the immigrant child for whom language is the greatest difficulty in the task of living in a new way. I am impressed when visiting schools in Melton Mowbray, Leicestershire, at the way in which, since the war the Polish people have become integrated with the population. When I said this to residents and teachers in the town, they replied that this was of course because they "are like us", "they look the same as anyone else". The language problem has been surmounted even though some of the children still come from homes where English is not spoken in general conversation.

Efforts are being made to ensure that the coloured immigrant children are dispersed over the school population. The imminent circular from the Department of Education and Science is thought to set a limit of about 30 per cent on the number of immigrant children admitted to any one school. A much higher percentage is, however, already existing in some places. In London and Birmingham some schools have over 50 per cent of coloured children. It is a difficult task to limit the number. The human situation is such that coloured immigrants tend to live in overcrowded conditions in a particular area of a city and the white people

* *Ibid.*, p. 75.

tend to move away. Some authorities are providing special buses to "siphon" these children to other areas. This tends to leave empty classrooms in the immigrant areas which are ill afforded at this time. It ought to be possible to have especially small classes and extra teaching staff to help with the problem of bringing immigrant children up to the level of learning of English children. Efforts are being made with the teaching of English, using special teaching in small groups, teaching aids, and machines.

It is important that the immigrant children are merged with the brighter English children. This is the surest way of preventing large-scale subnormality among immigrant children and a subsequent major problem for this country. At this time it must be accepted as a special problem in education, but it would be unwise to crowd special classes and schools for children with learning problems with immigrant children needing mainly language help and time and experience to adjust to a new pattern of life. English children need also time and opportunity to accept these immigrant children whose habits and customs may vary from their own and who need their help in communication. At the moment there is necessity for special resources to meet the particular needs here.

One must face, however, the fact that there are special social problems for the immigrant child which lead to there being a number of such children in schools and classes for the educationally subnormal. The housing situation for immigrant families is very bad indeed. There is indoor overcrowding and lack of outdoor space because the houses are most often in densely populated areas, such as Notting Hill, and the schools in these areas have little space indoors or out. So the children have little outlet for their physical energy, they are frustrated at school, their attainment being handicapped by social background and by language problems. Social problems do not show up so much until secondary age. Sex problems become intensified. The white community is much less tolerant of the behaviour of their coloured neighbours than of their white ones and, whilst they can find coloured children attractive and likeable, are very critical of the older coloured person. The parents find life difficult, and there may be family instability. Frustration occurs in competition with white people where employment is concerned. So there may be insecurity and maladjustment as a prominent problem in coloured immigrant communities. I recall the great insecurity of a mainly immigrant group from the Notting Hill adventure playground. We invited these children to be a "demonstration" class for dramatic work at a teachers' course. They held arms with one another in groups and lines for some time whilst moving as directed in the hall, until security came with absorption. Their drama was then lively and free. They were extremely successful in this medium.

"Mobile" Children

Occasionally one comes across a child in a school for the educationally subnormal because of the transitory nature of his education. Usually these children escape with their apparent subnormality and go from school to school as they move about the country. Their lack of learning is not a source of worry to their parents, and is only temporarily tiresome to teachers, but they very often remain illiterate.

One is reminded here of the very lively, verbally intelligent, confident children in schools such as the R.A.F. school at Cottesmore, Leicestershire, with which I am acquainted. These children are so experienced by their travelling and environment that their rapid changes in living and schooling result in rather excitable but freely communicative children, and certainly does not in my experience produce in itself subnormality.

I have tried to give a general but comprehensive picture of the kind of background from which some of the children about whom I am concerned, may come. School, however much it attempts to alleviate problems for these children, cannot solve entirely what may be the dilemma of belonging to a background. In the day school there can be constant conflict between home and school; in the residential situation there still remain the return at holiday times and at school-leaving age, and the conflict between the home as the residential child imagines it to be when he is away from it, and the school pattern.

Sensation—Sight and Hearing

Among the group of children with pre-natal, peri-natal, or post-natal damage must be included those whose hearing and or sight is impaired. These are very largely children who have less obvious problems in these two major sensory areas.

Difficulty in hearing in a child might remain undetected by a teacher with a large class and by unperceptive parents who meet the child constantly in the familiar set-up of the home. The detection of hearing defect is sought early where a child is recommended for special education, but it still appears to be just possible for a child to have hearing difficulties in his early educational years without a teacher or parent asking particularly for tests to be done.* Testing reported in *The Medical Officer*, no. 2956, by James A. Brown, a medical officer in Glamorgan (1964), involved 252 children who had been recommended for part- or full-time special education. Of these, 19 or 7·5 per cent were suspected of having defective hearing after an audiometric screening test. The 19 who had failed were given fuller tests and 16 failed these as well. Of these, 5 were judged later not to suffer from educational hearing loss. The 11 others were referred to an ear, nose, and throat consultant, and 4 of these were admitted to a class for partially-hearing children. Two of them have been fitted with hearing aids and three others go once a week to special lessons for those with hearing handicap. Only 3 are thought to be affected educationally, and the last child is waiting to go into hospital. There are some children who struggle in their learning with this enormous handicap, without recognition or help. A child not fully in touch with sounds, so that they are not meaningful to

* See footnote on p. 5, emphasizing careful screening. Babies at 8 months are usually screened, where contacted, for hearing disorder.

him, is most desperately worried and frustrated. His backwardness must be ever increasing, his apparent stupidity becoming more marked as his understanding of activity surrounding him becomes less.

Some of these children inevitably find places in special classes and schools for educationally subnormal children, where they receive special medical supervision, hearing aids if suited, and at last the understanding from their teachers which they have needed.

The point to be made here is the need for early diagnosis even when the hearing handicap is slight. These children are so severely handicapped in communication that their education must receive the utmost concern from the earliest possible moment.

There are in most special schools for children with learning difficulties some whose hearing handicap is associated with their subnormal ability, or for whom some degree of deafness is contributing to complicated learning problems. In the residential situation, particularly, there is opportunity for testing the adequacy of a hearing aid and for helping a child to become adjusted to it. Some parents are not sufficiently organized in their lives and homes or sufficiently understanding of the situation to encourage the child initially, to observe the nature of his difficulties and to help him through them.

A child may well have, as a result of his hearing difficulties, defective speech so that his contact with teachers and with other children is difficult and his progress further impeded. He may be suffering from aching or discharging ears, and if the latter, may be offensive to his neighbours because of the unpleasant smell. It may be that his deafness is associated with adenoidal and catarrhal conditions, adding yet more handicap to a child faced with learning the skills of language and making his early contacts away from home.

Sometimes certain frequencies of sound cause distress to children, especially to those with hearing disorder, and much in the world of sound disturbs and puzzles them.

All these children would be likely to be among those whom a

teacher might think backward, dull, and of low ability. They may be unattractive, withdrawn, and uncommunicative, candidates for low streams and special classes, or a school for the educationally subnormal.

It has been suggested that approximately 80 per cent of the work a child does in school is centred around close visual activity.* Sighted people depend largely upon vision for the accomplishment of work, for the activities of recreation and everyday tasks, and for necessary locomotion. Most of us find it easier to use our eyes than to use our ears, to watch television than to listen to radio. More and more visual aids are being brought into the classroom to augment the spoken word.

Visual defect is more common in children than any other except that of dental decay. In Liverpool in 1962, 314 entrants to the nursery and infant schools had defective vision and 158 others had some form of squint.

For a child who is totally blind or who has very little sight, the situation is a clear one, and, tragic as it is, that child will receive recognition and help as a handicapped person. It is important to consider the possibility of a child with slight impairment of sight having to begin school life under unrecognized difficulties, and the possible consequences of this. The ability to see properly is essential for a child if he is going to maintain normal progress in the infant school. A child might cope fairly adequately for a time where the programme is active and child-centred, but inevitably reading from charts and blackboards and from early reading books will soon present difficulties for such children, as confusion over letters and numbers arises. Many infant classes are very large; many teachers are inexperienced and stay only a short time in a school, often not becoming aware of the nature of each individual pupil. It would be possible for a child in spite of medical inspection to struggle for a time, becoming more and more frustrated and retarded without a teacher's recognizing that he was having difficulty.

Defect in vision can be associated with poor general health,

* *The Health of the School Child*, H.M.S.O., 1962 and 1963.

with malnutrition, or focal infection. It might well be associated with emotional disturbance as a causal factor or as a result of difficulty. It can also be symptomatic of very serious conditions such as diabetes or brain tumour.

A myopic condition could present problems for a child which would have long-lasting results to the detriment of his learning. A myopic child sees often clearly at close range and can cope with vision at short distances without accommodation. He could for a time resist those activities needing longer range vision, and even resist the wearing of spectacles after they had been prescribed, because whilst they would help him to see clearly more distant objects, they would bring about the need for more effort on his part to effect accommodation at close range. Here there could begin a pattern of frustration and resistive behaviour which would bode ill for a child beginning his school life.

A child with neglected poor sight can suffer from headaches and develop poor posture. His defective vision can influence behaviour, interfering with concentration, participation, and the whole area of personality development. Such a child may be pale, stooping, withdrawn, and unsuccessful. He may have a squint, he may be clumsy and badly balanced in physical skills, and a failure at games. He is not likely to be one of the most attractive or popular children in the class.

Eyes change with growth, difficulty in seeing could come about after the child had been examined by the school doctor, difficulty in seeing could account for deterioration in a child's work at school. Obviously the certainty that sight is not impaired, temporarily or permanently, must be part of investigation at an early stage whenever a child is falling behind in school work or in games activities.

Many of our children do spend their lives from early days coping well and naturally with defective vision with the aid of spectacles and regular medical care. They are ordinary children, individuals who have a handicap to overcome. Teachers are ready to help here and to avoid further strain for the children, even if they are less aware of the difficulties which these children may experience in balance, in physical skills, and in their every-day tasks. Many of these children come from homes where there would be little observation of a child's close work, and little awareness of other physical disabilities which might affect sight detrimentally. Parents can even be ignorant enough to be obstructive and to cause the child, by their stupidity and lack of understanding, much suffering and frustration. There were two cases in the same remedial class recently. The first was one in which the child wore her mother's glasses, having broken her own, "Because they both had the same eyes". The mother of this child said "She would not wear those National Health glasses you see". The second was the case of a child who needed glasses badly, having a severe squint, but who had none and who, ac-cording to her father, needed none, having caught the squint when she had been to play with another girl.

Mongol children, whom one occasionally finds progressing well in schools for the subnormal children, often have difficulties of sight with which to contend in addition to their other handi-caps. Many children in these schools have some degree of squint, from many causes, both physical and emotional.

The Sense of Smell

The sense of smell contributes to the sharpness and vitality of life. Its curtailment is a deprivation of a sensation which contri-butes to consciousness of the nature of things, and such depriva-tion is reflected in the use of language and in understanding. What, however, is most important in this instance is that the child whose sense of smell is impaired is likely to be the child whose breathing passages are blocked by catarrh or adenoidal growth, and who, because of this, is in poor health, tends to have an open mouth, defective teeth, to look dull, and to feel apathetic.

Linked closely with the sense of smell is that of taste. Here again loss is a lessening of the richness of living, a cutting short of experience, a diminution of language material.

Touch, Movement, and Kinaesthetic Sensation

The areas of sensory awareness which are neglected in education and in life are those which are connected with touch, movement, and kinaesthetic sense. Most normal active people are insensitive bodily. Training of these senses does not rank highly among the demands of the school curriculum, and few teachers recognize the value of allowing and encouraging children to touch, to feel, and to use their hands directly with material. Fewer still recognize the value of bodily sensitivity, that inner understanding of body position and body parts, the relationship of one part to another and the sheer aliveness and awareness of the skin, the joints and muscles, and the movement capacity of the whole body in touch with the space around it.

Children are often so enveloped in clothing. Sometimes the clothes are ill fitting and there are too many layers. Shoes are often hard and fit badly so that the feet become insensitive. Cold is a factor which causes the body to become tense and in-turned, cramped and unaware. Clothes can be insufficiently warm in the damp cold days of late autumn and winter. One sees, particularly, girls in cotton dresses, with legs uncovered, and plimsolls or thin shoes when the weather is bitterly cold, even in this age of considerable financial security for the majority. Sometimes children, in spite of school meals and milk, are poorly nourished and circulation is not good enough to keep the skin warm and glowing and the mind and body lively. All these factors, together with lack of rest and comfortable home conditions and a sense of security and happiness, can bring about a condition of lowered vitality, or sluggish bodily functioning and lack of sensitiveness, together with an adversity to normal healthful activity.

There may be pathological reasons not readily diagnosed which contribute to a general state of sluggishness in this area of sensation. Any state of ill health, a condition of hypo-thyroidism, or obesity, are all examples of this.

The physically handicapped child is sometimes very obviously deprived of full bodily sensation by deformity or absence of a limb, by lack of movement ability, by the encumbrance of splints or supports, and by the sheer difficulty of locomotion and participation in full activity.

This rich world available to the senses of the skin, muscles, and joints of the body, usually associated closely with the sense of sight, is one which needs emphasis in our present education. We tend to deprive children of the keenness of the feeling of things, of air, water, of texture and shape to be handled, of balance, strength and delicacy, of suddenness and smoothness in movement and so much that is available without cost.

Teachers themselves are often unaware of these things and are too engrossed with those items of learning which can happen within the confines of the conventional classroom and which can be more easily measured.

Many children, especially the slower, the apathetic, and the handicapped children of all kinds, need stronger stimulation especially in this field, so that their experiences may be of the highest possible intensity for them, and can become contributory to life experience and to the material for the use of language.

It is not intended that the consideration of the whole area of the senses should be separated from other areas of activity or indeed that any of the areas under discussion can be thought of in isolation.

Sensory stimulation is obviously dependent upon environment, upon education, and upon the ability to absorb and organize experiences.

MY VILLAGE . . . BOLTON-ON-DEARNE

A large common village with common people, friendly
people and unfriendly people. Lovely sweet green grass
surrounding a wonderful school. Television aerials
crowding and cluttering the chimney pots. A life of
television. Cats and dogs barking and screeching.
A busy and bustling village in parts and quiet and
inanimate in others. I like Bolton in some ways and
hate it in others. I love its cool shady trees. I hate
its winding dirty road.

(A boy aged 10.)*

* A. B. Clegg (Ed.), *The Excitement of Writing*, p. 55.

DEAD ROOT

The surface of the root is like dry, raked soil
Or the fossil of a prehistoric animal.
When slowly moved it is all shapes
And is crispy and bulky to touch.
It is rough in the ridges and gnarled.
The colour is greeny blue
And Flour-white with grey.
There are touches of yellow, orange and brown,
And it looks like a man's mouldy brain.

(Another boy aged 10.)*

I quote from the free writing of primary school children—children whose senses are sharp. These particular children come from a part of the West Riding of Yorkshire, which one might not expect to awaken the keen awareness of sensations, but rather perhaps to numb them. Stimulated by their pleasure in writing, they have brought to consciousness what they see, hear, and feel in their surroundings, and we see how vividly their senses are awake, and how meaningful sensation is to them.

It is without doubt a major task in education to "train" the sensory equipment of children. This is being well done by the teachers of pupils who write as those quoted above. Children are curious, interested, and keenly aware naturally, unless some defect of body or mind serves to impair or dull perception. Environment can be such that senses are dampened rather than enlivened: the climate of school learning can be such an environment.

The ability of the senses to function fully depends upon an environment that is rich. The world of the town-born child, that of people, noise, colour or lack of it, the smells and smoke of industry, the shapes and rows of chimney stacks, the occasional relief of a park, is rich in sense provision if the senses are awake. I remember in a London fog being able to smell my way down a road in East London which had a paint factory and a sugar refinery at one end and a soap factory at the other. The country provides other sense stimuli, perhaps of a quieter, more sustained nature, less cluttered and confused than those of the bustling town.

* *Ibid.*, p. 47.

Our primary schools in particular have realized the importance of feeding the senses. The growth in importance of the visual arts and of music has played a large part. The growing imposition of radio and television upon daily life has both enlarged the environment and dulled the awareness.

Some teachers are realizing the importance of kinaesthetic awareness, of bodily sensitivity, and the sense of touch; but these are senses which remain in most only partly awakened.

What, then, of the children for whom one or more of the sensory capacities are limited or lost before birth or later in life? Here is a very definite group of people for whom education is more difficult, for whom compensation is essential. "One sense may be substituted for another as a means of comprehension and of intellectual culture."*

Other senses do take over the function of missing senses and do make up to some extent. One sees the acutely sensitive awareness in the finger tips of the sightless person, the sharpened visual behaviour of the deaf person. This extra sensitivity arises not only through use and necessity, but through conscious and subconcious training.

There is the problem of the child who has a partially functioning or poorly functioning sensory capacity. It is important to use the remaining function to augment other senses and to use to the full valuable time for intellectual development. This problem arises, for instance, where there is partial hearing loss, where a child uses sight rather than struggle with his partial hearing capacity.

It is essential to study in some further detail the areas of sensory deprivation. Some are clear cut, as in total blindness existing as a single handicap; others are more generalized and less tangible, as in widespread hypo-tonia in hypo-thyroidism and in the generally decreased sensory sharpness which may occur in the ill nourished, the disturbed or deprived child, and for these and other ill-defined reasons in the so-called subnormal children.

* B. Hermelin and N. O'Connor, *Speech and Thought in Severe Subnormality*, p. 25.

In this study the accent will be upon those children who have diminution of sensory capacity rather than total loss, those for whom the whole sensory apparatus is dulled.

There must be concern also that the whole area of education of and through the senses is used to capacity, especially for children who are failing in our ordinary schools. This means the provision of a particularly stimulating environment, and teachers who are themselves awake and finding joy and interest in things around them and who understand the importance of educating the senses as vigorously and yet as delicately as possible in all children, but especially in children for whom learning is difficult.

Absorption, Recognition, Comprehension and Retention

> The central nervous system differentiates both structurally and functionally during the early years of life. At the outset its functions as a reflex organism capable of simply transmitting stimuli along predetermined courses to stipulated motor expression (an almost one to one stimulus response system). It then develops progressively through a series of levels permitting perceptual and finally conceptual function to ensue. At these higher levels signals are carried along specific input modalities, decoded and encoded, recognized, comprehended, retained in memory, associated with previously received stimuli and sensory images, in other words, they go through a process of integration before they become motor patterns along specific output modalities.*

The ability of a child to deal with that which he perceives, that function which we usually term intelligence, is the most intangible of these areas, the most difficult to examine, and the most entangled and confused with other issues. We have most often to have as a starting point a supposition about what is happening or failing to happen inside the mind of a child. We can judge by his reactions the evidence of his inner functioning, and if what we find suggests that something is wrong or inadequate, we can try to test all other areas for fault and then judge how much of the malfunctioning may exist in the mind.

There is, of course, a great deal investigated and known about the structure of the brain and the relationship between damage

* K. Herman, *Reading Disability*, p. 184.

and dysfunction, but where we are dealing with children who do not exhibit clearly symptoms of brain damage as the spastic child does, a great deal of experiment is necessary to discover where the limitation lies and how severe this is. There may be limited neurological functioning which makes for inability in a child to integrate ideas. Often there must be a limit to the level of intelligent behaviour we can expect, but in all cases one can be optimistic and set out to lift the level as high as possible by teaching and by enriching all other areas.

Because of the mystery lying behind so much backward behaviour in school, all areas must be explored and never must a child be given up as hopelessly backward. Always the emphasis should be on exploring the ability which is evident and on "feeding" with all resources possible. "The mind is an active, dynamic process by which a man interprets, integrates and manipulates his environment to satisfy his personal needs."*

Such activity requires effort and vitality on the part of a child and the desire and incentive to make such effort. Here the teacher can play a very large part.

> We often talk as if pupils were so many jugs to pour knowledge into, with the saturation point predetermined by the I.Q. . . .
> She asserted that she developed many of the best students from among those who were supposed on the basis of I.Q. to be incapable of superior work. I fear that a low I.Q. sometimes serves as an excuse for poor teaching.†

A sixth-form boy, talking about choosing A-level subjects, said: "I think the best way is to look around at the teachers and see who can teach, then take those subjects and hope they do not leave before you have finished."

This kind of thought absorbs me when I visit classes for backward children and the E.S.N. schools. Some of these children are taught by dedicated people; but others are given up by their teachers. Quite obviously there are immense difficulties and one cannot hope that with brilliant teaching and dedication children

* *Ibid.*, p. 179.

† Quoted from B. Shoesmith, a teacher of mathematics, by J. H. Hildebrand, *Is Intelligence Important?*, p. 6.

with major learning difficulties will become highly intelligent and skilfully functioning members of the community. But this book is dedicated to the cause of children who are in our schools for educationally subnormal children and in special classes. They need an attitude of optimism and care from teachers who believe in their ability to educate them.

Communication

We live in a culture where communication takes place primarily by means of the spoken word, a language which most children absorb from earliest days. Those who find the language of words difficult—the deaf, the stammerer, the child who for various reasons does not absorb the meaning of words or find it easy to use them, or the child who has begun life speaking in another tongue—for all these, communication, in our culture and especially in education, is very difficult. It is not only a question of being understood, of the necessary things of life, but of the expression of emotions and ideas and of the whole relationship with society. Frustration in communication is a major ill and must be at the core of our effort to overcome difficulties for children who are in special education.

Associated very closely with speaking are reading and writing. When the deaf child has mastered comprehension of the written word a great hurdle is overcome and communication with the world of books is available if that child has adequate brain functioning. So much is this so, that we see students at colleges of higher education for the deaf, such as the Gauladet College in Washington, D.C., mastering studies at a high academic level.

Let us consider the other means of communication which are available. Human beings use gesture, however small, to augment or emphasize their speech, or as a means of expressing ideas when speech is inadequate or not possible. The deaf find a natural form of expression in gesture. The world of gesture, exploited and expanded, symbolically, becomes dance, and gesture is dramatic expression. We must include, then, communication through

movement, dance, mime, and dance-drama. Poor body co-
ordination, lack of movement ability generally, may frustrate
here, but everybody has a power of movement in parts of his body
and sometimes this faculty is a very live one offering very full scope
for the expression of ideas. The body is a ready-made instrument.
The language of movement is an innate one. It need not be
intricate, yet can be developed to become a highly complex,
co-ordinated art. Later the use of movement for children who find
the language of words difficult will be fully investigated, to estimate how this mode of communication can be used to enrich, to
satisfy, and to help the acquisition of word language.

Communication can be through the manipulation of materials,
for most people, most often, through the use of the hands, painting,
modelling, sewing, carving, etc. In these ways children can
succeed in expressing their ideas and in discovering the world of
manipulative material. They need to make and to shape things,
and here is a way hampered only by a lack of manipulative
skill in some, which need not deter the exploration of this world
if there is a tolerant, caring teacher, who is prepared to allow the
children their way of creating, however simple or primitive it may
be, and to help them, if necessary, to fulfil their ideas. If a child
can paint or model what he is feeling or thinking about, it is
possible that words are not far behind.

Rhythm, sound, and music can play a prominent part in the
world of communication for the child for whom words are difficult. The language of music is a complicated one, but the body
has deeply rooted rhythmic qualities, and the manipulation of
simple musical instruments is possible for most children. There is
the whole world of musical sound for listening, to enrich environment, to sponsor ideas, and to increase the area of experience.

Communication is a two-way affair. We must be concerned
that a child expresses his ideas as fully and as freely as is possible
with a minimum of frustration, and that in communicating he
comes to organize and to understand them. We must also be concerned that he becomes a person with whom others can communicate: that he learns to comprehend.

I repeat, in this culture, the use of words is very important, and through all available means of communication the spoken and written word must be a language which we try to bring to these children. Therefore it is not only very important that means of communication, acting, dancing, music making, listening, painting, modelling, and the visual aid are all used as fully and skilfully as possible, but that they are used to assist the development of word language.

To be able to express ideas children must have them, and here one's thoughts return to the environment, the senses, and the mind. In this world of expressive media a teacher must be intelligent about the arts, understanding and appreciating their nature, but she must also be tolerant and encouraging, seeing through the daubing and the clumsy gesture that which to a particular child is meaningful and real.

CHAPTER 2

SCHOOL SURROUNDINGS
FOR THE LESS ABLE CHILDREN

It is necessary to make some brief observations about the buildings which house educationally subnormal children and the rooms which they occupy as special classes in ordinary schools. In a later chapter the "rich environment" for these children will receive greater attention.

The situation in the ordinary school is often the most difficult. This department is part of the whole, yet at this present time in secondary education there is a need for different material provision for these particular children. A teacher of a special class in a large secondary modern school, who had had experience in teaching primary children and saw how relevant some of the practical teaching methods were to the needs of her senior girls, talked to me about her desire to have a cooker, a sewing machine, painting space, and other "activity" materials in her classroom. This would be contrary to the pattern in the school where specialization was strong. How was she to give her girls the "doing" experience which she knew to be necessary and yet to avoid making them feel different or being called "infants" by the rest? Where the specialist facilities can be used, quite obviously this in the ordinary school is good, but so often there is a shortage of such facility which has to be fairly shared. Some specialists have little knowledge of, or sensitivity for, the teaching of less-able children, and if specialists are used a great deal there does follow the need for a more rigid time-table. It is essential that not only are specialist facilities, gymnasium, playing fields, domestic science department, art rooms, and hall space as available as fully as possible for these children, but that the classroom itself is large and generously equipped, leading the way perhaps for all classrooms to be so furnished and for a school to have more open and communally used space. In the junior school there is less likelihood of the children feeling different, but it is important that they have more than their share of any practical facilities.

Unfortunately one does find too often the special class tucked away in a small room, not receiving a fair share of the hall or gymnasium because school plays and practices in which they too often take no part, are being held.

In special schools, both residential and day, one finds great contrast and variety in conditions. There are some very old, drab buildings which the special school has been allocated as a makeshift measure. There are large, old houses, some homely and attractive, some ugly, some very inconvenient. There are large mansions with extensive grounds, with stables, and often a lake, and there are a few new buildings, built especially for this purpose. Some are very like institutions, some are very lovely, large homes. The school conditions most often reflect the attitude, care, and taste of the head and staff, including domestic and maintenance staff. Women heads most often take care with the colours and materials in dormitories, common rooms, and play rooms. Dining conditions are with a few exceptions more carefully planned and more civilized than in most ordinary schools. One could be critical and appreciative of most from one or more angles, but on the whole the best is made of conditions which are sometimes very difficult. The most general criticism which might be made is that there are so many schools where there is no good-sized indoor space. Often there is park land and garden, but very little space for indoor activity.

The schools are often a very long way from other people, from towns, and sometimes even villages. This seems a pity, but in view of the use made of country mansions for schools, is inevitable. It is obviously good that the senior girls in Halstead can walk unescorted up the road into town to buy some stockings for a teacher.

These schools do not need to be extremely elegant or expensive, but they do need to be homely, practical, and pleasant, to provide also a very rich environment for children, many of whom might be said to be suffering from environmental and stimulus starvation. As this rich environment is so closely connected with activity, it is sufficient to make this statement which will be clarified and extended when dealing with the actual developmental and learning situation.

An important point which needs to be made is that a school should not have a board labelling it ". . . E.S.N. School". We have not yet educated the general public, children, and adults, sufficiently. We still have adults who regard with horror, parents with shame, and children with ridicule, those who attend such schools. When a special school is on the same campus as an ordinary school, the staffs must and can take the opportunity of re-educating their small societies into a right attitude towards the children across the playground.

The special school on the same campus or near to the ordinary school is no doubt preferable to the situation which often exists, whereby the special school for the slowest learners is near to the training centre or on the same site as what used to be called the mental colony. The problem of siting schools is difficult, and ultimately what must be achieved is the re-education of attitude towards handicap and the acceptance of the fact that the term "ineducable" is not applicable to the children in schools which are at the moment not under the control of the education services. No child is beyond education. There are always faculties to be awakened and developed and there is ample evidence to prove how worth while it is to take a positive view, however hopeless a situation may appear to be. We must not allow such an attitude of defeat and negation of human dignity to continue.

CHAPTER 3

FAILURE

A man may put the blame upon the political or economic system, he may think people have a grudge against him, he may magnify some trivial physical defect, and hold it accountable for his short comings, or he may just curse his luck. One way or another he will bear witness to the perennial truth that man is never satisfied with himself.*

Everyone has experience of failure. It is impossible to judge its measure because it is set against so many factors of circumstances and personality. When talking to people about their failures a variety of attitudes emerge. Many speak immediately of financial failure. This has been obviously hard hitting and clear cut. Public failure can be overwhelming involving as it does revelation and a sense of shame. Few blame themselves for failure but many accept it as necessary for experience and learning.

As Malcolm Muggeridge once said, "First-rate pursuits court failure", and he quotes such self-avowed failures as Tolstoy, Shakespeare, and Christ. One has then to balance failure against the might of the task in hand. Some tasks are immeasurable, and full success is impossible to meet clearly, as the task of living a Christian life to the full, or of understanding the nature of the universe. Smaller and more practical tasks make success and failure easier to measure.

Failure can be a painful emotion which is associated with intense loneliness. Its impact upon a person depends so much upon the strength, vitality, and courage which he has at the time, and his ability to understand the failure, to come to terms with it, and to profit by the experience. Its effect depends also upon counteracting measures, balancing successes or alternatives, upon

* M. C. V. Jeffreys, *Mystery of Man*, p. 4.

love and security in human relationships, and acceptance in society.

With failure can come fear, guilt, and a diminution of dignity and self-respect. Shame and disgrace are potent weapons; they are states which destroy vitality and creativity, and only with great strength and resilience in a person can they contribute towards a courageous outlook and attitude. One has to be a very mature and secure person before one can accept failure in large measure and benefit from it, before one can be wary of success, becoming one of "those who grasp in full humility the fallacy of success, who are like the poor, blest".*

What part does our educational system play in the balance of failure and success? How far-reaching is educational failure in the life of a child? In school success usually means acceptance and being looked upon with favour by teachers; failure often means blame and rejection. At home, for some, this attitude is perpetuated, for others, there is passivity or active opposition to school criticism. From the latter home there is no furthering of censure, but there is no drive nor urging to greater effort in a child. Rejection, when ties are close, by parents and sometimes by teachers, can be especially painful.

Children should have vitality and great pleasure in life, excitement and joy in discovery and in learning, sufficient to overcome small failures. Physical health is a factor in child vitality, and even a short span of lessening of physical well-being might initiate educational failure.

School intelligence is of a special kind. It is the intelligence which involves writing, answering questions quickly, and responding to tests and problems. We place much emphasis upon a child's achieving "normal" intellectual standards. Children must not be stupid and "stupidity", a contemptible quality, is correlated with an inability to acquire normality in school work. It might have been related to a lack of strength, lack of inherited wealth, or lack of religious piety, but here it is literacy, and the acquiring of school skills which are important. It is quite obvious

* Malcolm Muggeridge, broadcast talk, B.B.C., September 1965.

that if a child is physically handicapped he is not the subject of ridicule by the well-behaved citizen, but if he is stupid he invites ridicule.

It is by comparison that a child can fail in school. The individual normal growth of the child is not that by which he is measured, but by that which the educationalists and teachers consider to be normal at the time. Teachers raise the standards of the normal as soon as they are approached by the majority, and think of failure as an absolute. What does a teacher mean when she says "Don't be stupid"? Once a child is labelled stupid it is almost impossible for him to escape from this label. Every mistake or hesitation he makes is put down to his stupidity.

Pupils differ markedly in the capacities which make up their learning abilities; their intelligence, special abilities, and disabilities, emotional responses, and social maturation, but if they differ markedly from what is considered normal there is danger of failure.

The child who is failing may respond by aiming too high or by satisfaction with too little according to his past experience and to his present measurement of himself. Children need the stimulus of success at any level, as well as the discipline of failure, otherwise they can become guilty and anxious, fearful of exposing incapacities. A child may try to avoid the pain of failure by deceit or truancy. Girls from a remedial class were found to become constant truants when dispersed into the fourth year in school. A child may become lazy, or may give up in despair, accepting his inadequacies. One cannot isolate the intellectual from the emotional, and the way to further educational failure is through maladjustment in the school situation. The ability to pay attention and the capacity to learn is acquired early, and inhibition here will be progressively effective.

If all children were equally able one could measure effort, but this is not so, and a teacher measures results. For some the goal is unattainable. Learning is often no longer important, only achieving the goal. Competition interferes with social attitudes and co-operative tendencies which are far more basic for living than competing.

At school a child is exposed to the chances of failure on all sides. Much failure is experienced in calculation and in language. There are the "new" subjects, such as French and science, which now compete with the old for places on the time-table. It is often important to the teacher that children succeed in these "new" subjects. A child can also fail so clearly and disastrously in some forms of physical education, even in music.

Frustration and anxiety are to some extent inevitable for every child, and they may contribute to development in a very positive way, but there must be balance, and such anxiety must be within a child's tolerance. Much of the motivation for learning stems from what Dr. Kelmer Pringle calls "normal anxiety", each individual having an optimum level of anxiety which to him is conducive to learning. Overstepped, this anxiety interferes with the learning process. "Most teaching problems stem from a super abundance of anxiety rather than a lack of it."*

A child's anxiety is brought about by what he thinks he ought to achieve. This pressure outside himself, not fully understood, may make anxiety deeper. His punishment is the cross, sad, disappointed, angry, even cynical or sarcastic parent or teacher.

There are children who are doomed to failure by their homes and backgrounds and by an educational system which puts them in a position whereby they are bound to fail. They become bewildered, defeated, and discouraged; there is a vicious circle of failure. These children are not guilty and cannot come to terms with their guilt feelings because they are not responsible. Neither can they come to terms with their fears. " 'My friend', said Father Vincent, 'your anxiety turned to fear and your fear turned to sorrow; but sorrow is better than fear. Fear is a journey, a terrible journey'."†

It is already too late for an emotionally deprived child to be

* Lindgren, 1956. Quoted by N. L. Kelmer Pringle in *Deprivation and Education*, p. 161.
† A. Paton, *Cry, the Beloved Country*, p. 102.

adequately prepared for schooling when he enters at 5 years old and we cannot yet control the genetic and environmental factors which prevent a child from being able to fit in with school demands. We can, however, meet the needs of these children in the schools, use our sensitivity and knowledge to find ways of avoiding some of the failures they encounter, and which enable them to develop as fully as possible intellectually, emotionally, and physically. We pay dearly for our lack of awareness of the nature of our schooling and for our preoccupation with achievement in the scale of learning. Even if proficiency in the skills of language and number were considered an adequate aim for the education of most children, certainly it could not be so for the child who does not fit our system, the educationally handicapped child.

CHAPTER 4

BEHAVIOUR PROBLEMS, MALADJUSTMENT, AND LAWLESSNESS

THE various problems which exist for the children we are discussing are bound to bring about for them difficulties in conforming to school life, and they often lead to anti-social and unacceptable behaviour patterns.

Let us consider first the residential school for educationally sub-normal pupils.

Many children are in residential schools for the very reason that their homes are not suitable places for them. In these schools the problems of individual children can be severe, and such children brought together are bound to provide difficulties for staff, especially where they are too few, too inexperienced, and are themselves living under strain. Many of these children are disabled because of their emotional instability, many suffer times of over-wroughtness and excessive excitability, and most are much more easily disturbed than the ordinary child. Such schools can never be completely settled in any one day. There must always be disturbing factors and difficulties of everyday life to be dealt with. It may be the epileptic fit, the child who did not get to the lavatory in time, or the child who has an "off" day. Going-home times before holidays provide setbacks, and equilibrium gained is constantly being broken down. There is need to take behaviour problems as part of everyday life, and this is exactly what happens in most residential schools. The tantrum, violent outburst, or misbehaviour is dealt with calmly and the incident does not unduly upset the atmosphere or working pattern.

Indeed, most of the residential schools for educationally subnormal children which I have visited have appeared to be very free from behaviour problems, even though I was told of the difficulties which had occurred. The security of the pattern of living and the acceptance of each child as an important member of the community brings about a relatively calm atmosphere. This is their school, they can be important here, and some of the competition is taken away. They are more likely to have sympathetic teachers who choose to teach them, not the least experienced or newest teacher. The whole atmosphere is more deliberately designed, the pace slower, the mood quieter, and with all this the children have less need to fight.

These children are excessively friendly, wanting desperately to hold hands with one, to touch and stroke, to be personally attended. This does not constitute a behaviour problem, although it can cause disruption. It is a natural thing when one considers that these children are away from the personal affection of home and parents and that most of them have had less than their fair share of individual love. This need for bodily contact, the aggressive demand for personal attention, and the great desire to serve, is a practically unvarying pattern of behaviour in residential schools of this kind. It does present difficulties for overworked staff with many children in their care; they do sometimes become hardened and slightly cynical under the weight of this problem, but there are many who maintain a kindly, parental affection for all their charges. As one would expect, the "affection" problem is most obvious in junior schools and in schools for senior girls, although we may too readily disregard the needs for tenderness of older boys.

Where behaviour problems of a severe nature do exist in a residential situation there are fairly obvious reasons. The personalities of staff, combined with inadequacy of their numbers or with material difficulties, make demands impossible for them; numbers are too large for a single school of this nature, or there are included too many major problems of instability or maladjustment.

Special day schools for educationally subnormal children share many of the characteristics of the residential school, and in spite of the fact that there must be some conflict with the home environment for some children, and therefore added chance of disturbed behaviour, there appears to be little severe behavioural problem here.

The problem of controlling in order that work may take place is most serious in the special classes and lower streams (where no special classes exist) of the secondary school. This is where there are extreme difficulties; where a young teacher finds it almost impossible to relax sufficiently into the working situation for any adequate period of time and becomes tense, fearful, and concerned only that a modicum of good behaviour appears to be taking place. One can feel nothing but sympathy and care for such a teacher, often a very inexperienced young person straight from a college of education. Indeed, it is disheartening to see a lively, young teacher ashamed and humiliated at failure, dispirited, and resorting to methods which she sees being used around her, which her colleagues, only a little more experienced than she herself advise, and which superficially appear to "work". It is not very helpful to try to persuade her that these are the very methods which contribute to her difficulties. One advises gentleness, care, understanding, and patience, yet one knows that in such an environment, isolated among the shouting and disapproval, these cannot work in time to rescue a young teacher from using other methods in self-preservation.

Behaviour problems in schools in our more poorly endowed areas of large towns exist most surely in these classes, but even here the degree of problem varies very much from year to year. So marked is this variation that one must look beyond the accident of teacher changing and variations in material conditions. It would seem that it often occurs because of the nature of the strongest personalities within the class. The groups of children, varying as they do in their individual difficulties, are very susceptible to the influence of their strongest members, as they are also susceptible to the mood of these members. The disturbance in equilibrium of one child can easily cause general bad behaviour. The teacher of a class with whom I have been closely associated would say, "They are in a bad mood today. You see A's mother has left the family yesterday."

One finds, of course, a school in an area where there are many unstable and deprived homes, but where there is order and relative peace and dignity, because there is a head who radiates over a length of time such a pattern, and who has loyal members of staff, so that the aura and mood of the school permeates, giving security and direction to the young recruits to the teaching staff.

It is difficult sometimes to identify the causes of behavioural differences in our schools, but most often the difficulties—or lack of them—depend upon the tone set by the head, if this is supported by the influential members of staff, remembering also that a head sometimes inherits an extremely difficult situation. Some of the biggest problems arise where the head has progressive educational ideas, but where the strongest personalities on the staff do not agree and spread an atmosphere of distrust between the head and the staff. It does happen, of course, that a head who has the welfare of pupils at heart, is full of sympathy and care, and has good educational ideas, does not really understand the difficulties which the staff are encountering, and most of all does not know the staff well enough to realize their difficulties. This kind of head does not really encounter the classroom situation. He talks to badly behaved children kindly, seriously, extracting from them promises of effort and good behaviour, but he does not reckon with the relationship between the child and the class teacher and does not fully appreciate his own privileged position as the understanding head. So one hears in schools teachers who have little confidence in their head; "He does nothing to help, it is no use, he only talks to them." One hears this kind of remark so often and wonders what it is that the teacher wishes the head to do. Meanwhile the head waits for the day when he will receive teachers who can work his way; but the disruption of work, the strain on the young entrant to teaching, and the negative quality of the education for the less able child go on.

There is one remedial class in each year; each contains about 25 boys, few of whom can read. The first and second years are treated like inadequate children. The third year is transitional, as they begin to realize their true position. By the time they reach the fourth year, fourteen turning fifteen, only the toughest available master can cope with them. If ever we have a compulsory fifth year, the logic of our present system will suggest that we must find a tougher master still.*

Some special classes have an atmosphere of happiness and security. The children work with obvious effort, willingness, and enjoyment. These classes can exist even where a school atmosphere is one of rough behaviour and lack of effort. This happens only, however, where the teacher or teachers in the department are of very good calibre and are very well led, giving to the children special care and a special place of importance, shielding them with a measure of protection.

In special classes in junior schools bad behaviour is less prevalent. These children have not been so long rejected, or their efforts so long frustrated. Teachers of primary school children, because of their training and the fact that they wish to teach young children, may find it easier to understand the difficulties involved. The work is more child-centred in attitude so that a child can, on the whole, work at his own pace and less boredom occurs. In any case the anti-school, anti-social aggressive behaviour which can occur in senior classes has not developed to the same degree and the strains of adolescence have not usually begun.

Where junior classes are difficult, however, there can be great frustration and tremendous strain for the teacher. The junior child is usually very lively physically, and the teacher trying to curb outbursts of activity and aggressiveness can increase disturbance and unco-operative behaviour.

The problem of behaviour difficulties is then great enough to be of special concern in any discussion of the teaching of educationally subnormal children. Many of the reasons for the problem are quite easy to see.

* A young teacher writing on "A neighbourhood school", *New Society*, June 1966.

In the case of younger children especially, special classes are often too large. The children have such individual difficulties that they need attention devoted to them singly or in very small groups. The emotional climate of these classes can only be tolerated if disturbance is kept at a minimum, and this can often only be done in some circumstances by repressive measures and by great strain upon a teacher. Unfortunately one does find that in an effort by heads to give teachers a little extra time to themselves, groups are put together for practical work such as physical education, drama, dance, and the situation in these exciting activities becomes impossible if one believes in exploring ideas and in creative work.

In many ways the stresses suffered by educationally subnormal children are greater than those of the mentally defective child. The children we are discussing are not succeeding for varying reasons, and they can be vividly, shamefully aware of failure. The educationally subnormal child is more blameworthy than the mentally defective child because he is not so obviously handicapped. Frustration for many children labelled educationally subnormal must be very great indeed because they are often within sight of success. These children have failed so much, some for as long as they can remember, some at school only, others also at home, and in their play groups. They need to be accepted by their group at least. A child will go to great lengths to be accepted. So we get anti-social behaviour, hostile attitudes, destructiveness, and leadership by the aggressive children who are the trouble makers. Children may withdraw and be unco-operative; moods are common; anti-authority feelings can predominate. These children can be anti-school, anti-rule, and anti-parents in their effort and need to assert and establish themselves as being of importance. Nothing is "fair", they are angry, resentful, and defiant. Such feelings result in noisy, tough behaviour, fighting, and the destruction of things for which they may care. Sometimes the kind of behaviour which exists between children and parents at home is quite unacceptable at school. They are probably used to rows, drunkenness, bad language, and uncontrolled anger. Their restlessness and resistance to discipline dictates their attitude to school. This kind of behaviour shocks teachers, yet when one investigates one can often see the reasons for the storm and one wonders if such understanding could not precede and perhaps prevent the outburst.

A girl in a special class, having learned some part of the words of a play in which she had been given a role, had it taken from her, the casting having been revised because it was felt that she was after all too slow at learning her words. The whole class was affected by her anger and a locked door, the culminating factor in frustration, was kicked in. Sometimes these children are on the edge of explosion, and it takes only a little more hurt to bring about a crisis. Their world is not genteel, and if angered and frustrated to extreme the result is physical violence.

> Schools are having to wage a perpetual war against attitudes created by doubtful adult habits and inventions—pools, bingo, alcohol, tobacco, striptease, sex in advertising, slot machine contraceptives, excessive wages, and the exploitation of violence by mass media.*

Many children must be in a state of utter confusion as they live in a world of commercial exploitation, parental weakness, and the expectation of teachers, that they conform to totally different standards.

These same children can be gentle and extremely kind, giving generously to a need, especially if that need concerns one of their own number and is one which they can appreciate. They are often loyal and very thoughtful as when warned that money used to mend kicked-in doors would leave less for buses to the swimming bath, they carefully cleaned all the desks of marks and scribbles to try to make up for the broken door which they could not mend. Moods of generosity and happiness are fortunately as infectious as the other rather more prevalent moods of aggression or non-co-operation. A wise teacher learns to accept, to go with, and where necessary to ignore moods which she cannot break through or use.

* Sir Alec Clegg, Conference of Urban District Councils' Association Blackpool, June 1966.

"What is wrong today? You do not join in", I asked a girl who had sulked through a drama session. "I am in a mood," said the girl. I answered, "It will pass away". "Yes, after a while it will", she answered politely.

Some blame for the problems of behaviour must rest with the conditions in which teachers and children work. As we have seen, so often the classroom is too small. The group might be the smallest group in a large secondary school, but it is a pity that they have as a result the smallest, pokiest, dark room which makes it very difficult for the display of pictures and charts, for active work to take place, or for the children to make their room attractive and interesting. There is not facility for the children to be individual and to possess their own materials. It is very important that they have possessions and that they can keep them safely. They are likely to be the children whose home environment is the most impoverished of those in the particular school and they are proved to be inadequate in dealing with their impoverishment, yet often the school environment provided is of a colourless, limited kind and the work attempted unlikely to stimulate them, interest them, and shake them from their rejection of schooling and near hatred of education as they have known it. The equipment is not right for them. When they make efforts the result is not rewarding. The classroom is geared to the needs of reading, writing, and number, and even where these skills are concerned the material does not cater for the older child who has not yet mastered them at an elementary stage. Learning is not for them very exciting. One cannot be very surprised if they do not come to it eagerly. So it is that energy emerges in other ways, as it would with the intelligent child if he were frustrated and bored.

Teachers, too, must take some of the blame although often they inherit a climate of behaviour for which they are not responsible. In some schools it is possible that the new teacher never receives a real opportunity to teach. Certainly there is no second chance if the initial stage of wonder is not used with some success. Nevertheless, many teachers set out to teach these children, listening to their colleagues' disheartening comments. They expect little in the way of achievement; they look for behaviour problems, guarding against them before they come. No risk is taken, no gaiety or excitement enters the work, and so the dull, restricting round continues, inevitably relieved by some outburst of rowdiness.

Teachers often do not understand their pupils; they are too far removed in their social and expressive attitudes. Often a remark made by a child sounding rude or even impertinent is not meant so and may be intended as a particularly friendly gesture. These children do not often possess the polished manners and habits which teachers somehow expect. Teachers like them sitting down, tidily and quietly, and suppress spontaneity and freedom of expression lest it should become something they cannot control.

The problem of the teacher who is to succeed with these classes is great, but at this moment we must recognize the teacher as being responsible for some aspects of difficulty where behaviour is concerned in special classes and less often in special schools for educationally subnormal children.

One cannot become interested in the problems of subnormality without becoming aware of the range of handicap which is involved and of other areas with different labels which impinge directly upon this one. One is concerned immediately with maladjustment. A child may be maladjusted without being educationally subnormal, yet his deviance from accepted behaviour may well lead to his inability to take part in learning situations. It would appear that in our society it is very difficult for a child to remain adjusted in a classroom situation if he is unable to keep up with an accepted rate of achievement and is unable to communicate at the required level. Whether subnormality precedes a measure of maladjustment, or whether a maladjusted state brings about apparent educational subnormality, is uncertain. There is without doubt, however, a strong enough link here to necessitate in this study some consideration of maladjustment as we use the term, and as a condition to be reckoned with when working with the so-called educationally subnormal child.

The maladjusted child has been described by Lord Kilbrandon as, "A child not accepting normal behaviour standards, but with adequate level of understanding; someone who insists upon doing something which is prohibited and out of step with society."*

This is the description given by one who is concerned with juvenile delinquents. He went on to add to this: "Those children in need of care and protection, those outside parental control, persistent truants, and all those children in trouble." One might talk about deviant children, those with ego disorders, the over anxious, affectionless, or unhappy child. One must be aware of the withdrawn child. These troubled, sad children are so often ignored because they cause no disturbance, whilst the noisy, delinquent child is urgently sent for help. The quiet, passive child who makes no effort can become increasingly maladjusted and backward whilst she disturbs no one. I deliberately say "she", because this factor of the ignoring of the least troublesome may account for some of the discrepancy between numbers of boys and girls in schools for the educationally subnormal and more markedly in schools for the maladjusted.

There is a danger in the labelling of children into categories— E.S.N., maladjusted, neurotic, psychotic. So often the categories are overlapping or interlocked and confused, and in any case a child needs to be considered as an individual, with unique difficulties, whose social environment must be made as normal as possible in order that he may adjust and be able to take a place in society. Children who are not emotionally "tough" are likely to be susceptible to stresses of many kinds.

> It would seem in short, that a certain number of children are born with a type of impairment to their nervous system which affects their behavioural stability. . . . Such children tend also to suffer from a wide range of other neurological defects, and also physical weaknesses which make them liable to respiratory and other diseases.†

* Conference of Association of Workers for Maladjusted Children, Edinburgh, August 1965.

† D. H. Stott, Why maladjustment?, *New Society*, December 1964.

Many more physically delicate children survive now with advances in medical science, and we have a large number of our children who are more vulnerable to emotional disturbance, maladjustment, and educational subnormality. The stress responsible lies in the home or less often in the school.

Children were brought under continuous observation by compulsory education and more acutely and individually by the institution of the school medical service. Progress in psychiatry has made it more possible for us to understand children's behaviour and deviance in learning progress. The 1944 Education Act made it obligatory for local education authorities to assess and provide for handicapped children. There is varying provision for the educationally subnormal, accounting to some extent for the great variation in ability and severity of handicap which one finds in the schools. For the maladjusted, the provision of special education is very limited. The children who do find places in special schools for the maladjusted may receive great care from a specialized and large staff, but only a few children receive resident protection and help. Clinics for the maladjusted child, within the hospital system, within the local education authority services, or joint clinics between the local education authority and the regional hospital board, do a great deal of therapeutic work, but there is need here for a much greater liaison between the psychiatric social workers, the clinic, and the school. Social workers with whom I have discussed these matters appear to have very little knowledge of the activities of a normal school and to resent the teacher as a co-therapist. There is evidence, too, of lack of co-operation on the part of the teachers to share their educational ideas, and a distrust of psychotherapeutic services.

There must be concern for the delay evident in bringing help to children where circumstances become such that stress is too great and for whom maladjustment, deterioration in educational attainment, and delinquency become an inevitable sequence. The legislation involved and lack of urgency is such that children who are unfortunate enough to lose a parent, are in the midst of parental separation or divorce, or whose home is the centre of some other disturbance do not receive adequate help early enough to save them from what would seem to be inevitable consequences. The account which follows illustrates this point very well:

When *A* joined the modern school, on 4 September, 1961 he was a normal lively boy. His primary school record card stated that his attendance at school had been regular and his health normal. His parents' choice of career for him at this time was that of an electrician, a recognition of their son's capabilities which his secondary school headmaster considered more realistic than many similar parental arrangements. English was his strong subject, estimated at 60 per cent with an 'A' for oral and a 'B' for written expression. His standard in arithmetic was given as 55 per cent and general ability 60 per cent. He had "normal" reliability, initiative, and persistence.

He was known to come from a good home, with a mother who was particular to see that her sons were well turned out and arrived on time for school. . . .

In form 1C *A* began quite well. At the end of the first term he was placed 19th out of the 32 boys in his form. This was not maintained.

His form master's comment on this state of affairs is of interest:

He was doing quite well in attendance and work until a family upset caused irregular attendance and lack of concentration. . . .

The "upset" was the departure of his father with another, younger woman. . . . The emotional violence thus brought upon the family was quickly seen in *A*'s appearance; where he had been clean and tidy before, his uniform was now unkempt and dirty. This reflected not only his own but his mother's distraction. . . .

His mid year report commented:

Has gone to pieces this term and if he had been present for the exams I doubt if he would have coped favourably with them. Due for medical report concerning his problems.

The headmaster summarized the case as follows:

A boy of above average ability, working well up to his second year, then father left home to live with another woman. Mother began slowly to crumple mentally, is now very unstable, but with intermittent bouts of clarity. Over the last two years the boy has developed school phobia, often hides in school huts on allotments near home; speaks of trying to get work to help mother but, in fact, never succeeds in doing anything but drift.

The report proceeds in detail to describe this boy's deterioration, but the point is that the administrator adds, "The point that worries me about all this is that pretty well every welfare organization that one can think of was brought to bear on *A*'s case, and nothing has had the slightest effect".

In this case sheaves of writing have been executed between headmaster, divisional education officer, divisional medical officer, children's officer, assistant children's officer, health visitor, and others between February 1963 and June 1966, when the writer of the document concerned ended: "The wheel has come full circle."*

The need of psychiatric help for the educationally subnormal child who is maladjusted can be even more difficult to obtain. Educationally subnormal children suffer often from multiple handicaps—emotional, physical, and social—and so often they need the help of a child guidance service.

Another aspect of maladjustment related particularly to educational subnormality is that of accident proneness. There is some evidence that children involved in accidents with frequency have a history of deviant behaviour or restlessness and distractable habits at school. They are often insecure children, compensating by assertion and over activity.

> The predisposing factors to accident involvement in children appear to be a stressful family background, an irritable, dominant parental attitude toward the child, and some degree of neural impairment resulting in inconsequential and restless behaviour.†

We should then, consider behavioural deviation even to the point of maladjustment of personality, as very likely to occur in the child who is educationally subnormal. It is important that these children should share the amenities available for the maladjusted, and that the teachers responsible are aware of the dual problem and the relationship between behaviour difficulties and inability to learn. Teachers of the educationally subnormal must be tolerant and understanding, making the climate of the school one which can tolerate different behaviour. Heads, administrators, and those concerned with advice and research into ways of helping these children, should be aware of the possibility of behaviour difficulties and of the limitations of teacher tolerance.

* This story has been taken from a lengthy and detailed report in an educational administrator's file of such cases in his area.

† L. Burton, The child in a road accident, *New Society*, May 1965.

When dealing with educationally subnormal children one is always considering the problem of a measure of maladjustment for some children at a particular time and endeavouring to find ways whereby stress situations may be avoided and whereby the children's individual problems may be dealt with.

How much does educational subnormality contribute towards delinquency? One might be wise here to substitute the term school failure for educational subnormality. I quote from a letter from an education officer of one of Her Majesty's Borstals:

> There are no educationally subnormal boys in this Borstal, and indeed no boys who are subnormal in any respect. The young men with us probably differ from the general run of people in their age group only in that they tend to be a little more intelligent than average. My own interests lie far more in the disparity between ability and formal academic attainment, and in attempting to make up as far as we can, for the damage which appears to be done to intelligent, sensitive people by clumsy, and unperceptive handling in conventional schools, secondary modern and secondary grammar. . . . What I can show you is evidence of maladjustment which has been increased, sometimes quite severely, by inadequately trained or unsympathetic teachers more ready to blame than to help their pupils.

One has also to consider the blanket term delinquency. This term cannot be taken to mean all those young people who transgress the sanctions of the law. Rather they are those who are caught doing so. Young persons who lack care for others, sympathy, generosity, integrity, and even honesty, do not necessarily belong to this group. They are those who are discovered in anti-social behaviour, breaking the laws made in accordance with a particular social evaluation, including truancy, sexual promiscuity, and running away from home. Nevertheless, there is a great responsibility resting upon education to investigate the relationship between school failure and law breaking, and to discover how children who are members of low streams, special classes, and special schools because they have learning problems, can be helped to become citizens who have healthy attitudes towards work and the society of which they form a part.

We must remember that children who are behaviour problems at an early stage in school are often placed in low streams, special classes, or even special schools, mainly because of this.

A delinquent person is a persistent offender, so that by the time he joins this category the way of life is to some extent established and it may well be too late to change successfully the trend of his energies. The need for early help and prevention of the activities which bring a youngster to court is emphasized by such figures as are available from follow-up studies of approved schools and borstals. These indicate the severe limitation of success of later education.*

The recovery of personalities at this stage is very difficult, the number of enlightened people to work in approved schools and borstals few, and the obstacles very great. The only solution to the problem of delinquency is social amelioration and education of the young child through thorough understanding and dedication by teachers of each individual child in their care, involving, of course, the need for small classes and excellent teachers. The majority of adult criminals begin anti-social careers as child delinquents.

S. and E. Glueck, in their book *Delinquency in the Making*, compared 500 delinquents with 500 non-delinquents. They state that nearly half the delinquents had shown evidence of delinquent behaviour before the eighth year, and another two-fifths before the eleventh year.

The strongest factor which is common to many educationally subnormal children and to many delinquent youngsters is that of social deprivation. Some learn about criminal behaviour at an early age, living in an environment where gambling, drunkenness, and immorality surround them. Early on they learn to "swipe" from counters, to "hop" trucks, to sleep rough, and to have little respect for law and order. They may admire and desire to emulate a father who "gets away with it" and does well. They may live in a neighbourhood where petty theft and vandalism are the laws of the streets. In such a neighbourhood a child learns early antagonism to authority, police, and school; material success is highly prized; poverty of living is demoralizing; home is an unpredictable place, without laws, without care, so that he

* Robert Shield, The guilt cage, *Observer*, 25 April 1965.

can stay out late and no questions are asked about actions, acquisitions, or friends. Decisions are made without thought for the future.

The cause of their early misbehaviour is partially in the environmental subculture and is essentially in the lack of security and decent living in the home. Some such children stand a slender chance of growing up to become adults who earn a steady, honest living, and tend a good home. School, too, has an almost impossible battle. The problem is essentially a social one needing the efforts of social, medical, and educational workers.

There is no doubt that many children who are behaviour problems outside and inside school are those whose school attainment is poor or becomes progressively poorer.

The social maladjustment of some children results in bad behaviour, unruliness, or refusal to accept school situations; then comes truancy and the searching out of more exciting and rewarding adventures. When one comes across the circumstances of home life which some children have to tolerate, one understands very well the reasons for their behaviour, indeed one wonders why they conform for so long and so well to the demands of ordered school life and the association with cleaner, better fed, more rested and more affluent classmates. The conflicts of discipline which these children face are sufficient to cause anxiety in the most adjusted child. Cigarettes may be given at home as a reward, whilst at school they are a punishable offence. Truancy is condoned by mother or father. Father says, "Don't take it from nobody", and at an early stage a child learns aggression.

How much can failure in school account for delinquency? In Glueck's study there was a striking difference in school attainment between the delinquent and non-delinquent groups; teachers stated that half the delinquent group and fewer than two-tenths of the non-delinquent group had lack of interest in school work. They reported more inattention, carelessness, tardiness, restlessness, and laziness among the delinquents than among the others. One could ask many questions concerning teaching methods, teachers' attitudes, and testing criteria, but there are nevertheless many children for whom school is unexciting, undesirable, and frustrating, who may have a poor relationship with teachers, and possibly with other children, who in their frustration turn to misbehaviour, and from there to delinquency in the world outside.

It is easy to see how vulnerable children are who fail in their school tasks to early deviation from accepted behaviour and how such deviation furthers the failure. Although many delinquents are by no means educationally subnormal, many have failed to achieve success in school, especially as they have reached the senior stage. Behaviour and scholastic achievement are inevitably related as closely as both are related to the attitude of the teacher towards a pupil.

One feels great sympathy with the child who in his frustration becomes self-pitying, angry, degraded by his failure, and hampered beyond measure by his background. These young people must not be further degraded, further frustrated, or made more to feel useless. They need social acceptance to enable them to establish themselves as personalities, and, most of all, so that they will be able to make relationships which will be helpful and sincere, forestalling harmful friendships which they come across so easily after commitment to a borstal or approved school.

We have to try to understand the position of children who fail so much, especially as they grow into adolescence and adulthood. The young male has so much frustration if he is handicapped in taking his place in the adult world. He must explode energies and so exhibits aggression which appears to be useless, perhaps even self-damaging, careless, irresponsible, and stupid.

Frustrations are necessary to education and to development, but they must be of the right amount and at the right time for the person concerned, and there must be clear solutions. Such children may be restless, self-assertive, defiant, suspicious, and hostile, and their frustration finds outlet in destruction, aggression, and acquisition. They may attempt to solve their conflicts through submissiveness, withdrawal, or truancy. These are children in great trouble and such children may well end up in the court of law. Often they are isolated, feel rejected, and inadequate. Craving acceptance they are ready prey for the stronger members of gangs and are easily led into behaviour which they may not even fully comprehend. The aspect of conscience and its restraining power is more remote for the deprived and poorly understanding child. He is equally lacking in restraint for his aggressiveness, and he tends to be impulsive, unable to persist through his own will and to make decisions. He expresses in physical terms which are so often unacceptable ones to society. Social pressures lead to delinquency.

It has been necessary to deal with this latter subject because it shows so clearly the tremendous responsibility which rests upon every teacher, but more acutely upon the teacher who receives the less able, the backward, or educationally handicapped child. These children are especially vulnerable. They stand a good chance of becoming transgressors of the law, aggressively criminal, followers and stooges for criminals, prostitutes, weak, immature, and craving affection, but, at school age, they are much more the victims of transgression.

CHAPTER 5

THE EDUCATION SYSTEM
AS IT AFFECTS THESE CHILDREN

WE MUST now look at the school experiences which a child may have, to find factors which contribute to the apparent and real subnormality of some children. What happens to human beings in the process of education in this country?

As we have seen, in nearly all our infant schools the atmosphere and the quality of teachers foster learning attitudes, using children's natural curiosity and vitality. We call such an approach progressive as opposed to the traditional. Concern in progressive education is for the whole of a child's development, for making an environment wherein for each child learning may take place. Neither the teacher's plan, nor the syllabus, nor marks, nor competition are stressed, but that which contributes to the development of the individual and his growth in every way in a social environment. Such an approach has developed in our infant schools over the last 30 years. Infant schools are, on the whole, so lively and so progressively educational that a child does have a chance to develop at his own rate and to remain relatively unhurt by frustration and failure. The classes are usually large and teachers are often inexperienced and lacking in deep understanding of the reasoning behind that which they do and of the situations which they sponsor, however, so a child who finds the early skills difficult could, even in the infant school, escape vigilance for a while, so that already he might be vulnerable for impending failure in the junior school. Our good infant schools do offer, however, opportunities for the child who is less able, has disadvantages of home or handicap of body which are minimal enough to enable him to take his place in such a community, and so it would seem extremely unwise for such children to be in a special school whilst still of infant age unless there were specially complicating circumstances in school or home.

If only every junior school could be a place where progressive education continues, it is possible that many more children could proceed in their education profitably and happily in the ordinary school. Some junior schools continue environmentally stimulating and child-centred education, keeping for children their joy in learning and their curiosity which excites the process, prolonging and stabilizing the "romantic" stage of learning which exists for every child. A good progressive junior school is one where learning inevitably meets the hurdles of necessary techniques, eases the way through with sensitive teaching, and leads smoothly and surely to the stage where skills can be used at each level. There are many schools where this is happening, but still more where, in keeping with outdated but somehow revered tradition, the "fun" is cut down and learning is "work", a not pleasant, yet necessary thing. In these schools the gaining of skill, memorizing, and testing are prolonged and accented. This has something of the atmosphere still which indicated that work, like medicine, must be nasty to be good.

This is where difficulties arise for the child who cannot keep up with the teacher. Like success, failure spills over into other areas and quite easily one can have a frustrated or bored child, unable to cope with the demands of the teacher, failing as a result to please parents if they are sufficiently aware, and failing to take a satisfactory place among his contemporaries; a child for whom life can become intolerable. The child who is not comprehending, who is slow or distressed, can never succeed in a system where marks and measurements are the criteria, earn praise and status, and therefore respect from fellows. These children have little choice whilst their difficulties accumulate, but to give up. The work is not shared as in the infant school. Such a child is alone in his predicament. To get help from his neighbour would not fit in with this system. Traditional teaching is centred upon a teacher's plan. Communication is limited to that between teacher and class, and it is mostly one way—from the teacher to the class. There is little chance for self-expression and for communication between the children themselves, little richness in relationship, little sharing one with another and with the bustle of the outside world. Children with existing learning handicaps cannot become involved in this traditional method and are doomed to failure and to further learning difficulty. How many more children develop learning problems because of teaching methods and approaches at this junior stage? Can we blame our own teaching for the educational subnormality of some children?

Teachers themselves, in their attitudes towards children, may very well contribute substantially to a child's frustration and lack of ability to keep up with his fellows. Without realizing the lack of justice and the irreparable damage done, teachers attach blame and false judgements to children who look ill kept, and are unattractive because of uncleanliness or unhealthiness. Children who come from a large family are often late for school because they have been running errands, they cannot stay behind to help or to practise for a play or athletics or games because there is a baby brother to take home. Such children tend to be thought of subconsciously perhaps as nuisances, not worth teacher's extra concern. These children often come from casually run, inconsistent homes where parents do not co-operate when the child is asked to bring a small sum for an outing or waste materials for craft work. Such parents are often hostile to school; the teachers are to them enemies and have been to their families for generations, there being a tradition of scholastic failure. A teacher may well expect further members of such a family to be tarred with the same brush. A sibling starts already with a disadvantage because of his family reputation. Instead of a child from an empty, discouraging home receiving extra incentive and encouragement, the situation is exactly reversed. It is well to remember here, however, that the less obviously able sister or brother of an older, bright, attractive child may well, after a short disappointing period, suffer severely by comparison from a teacher with his brighter relative.

It is very easy for a young teacher who is faced with the strain and emergencies of a large class to be drawn in affection and attention to the cleaner, well-dressed children, looking as she would wish her own children to look, who talk readily of their experiences at home, at weekends, and in the holidays, who bring flowers and nature finds, who respond to teacher's request for cardboard boxes, paper, or contributions for the Oxfam box, and whose parents visit on open evenings, showing interest and appreciation. Such a teacher can hardly be expected easily to realize the needs of the other children who are unresponsive, possibly badly behaved, and even aggressive. The contribution, however, made to failure in school for these children by the attitude of a teacher is considerable.

It is necessary to study more closely the qualities and attitudes of teachers and this will be done in another chapter. Here we should note the frequent changes of teachers in schools and the great contribution which this lack of stability makes to the insecurity of children whose homes offer little steadiness. We should note, too, the inexperience of many teachers who face large classes in areas where there is a preponderance of deprived homes. Their difficulties are great and too absorbing usually to allow for the special care and patience which is necessary for the less-privileged child.

We now have many primary schools where the children are not streamed according to ability but still a majority of schools where they are. In larger primary schools where there are two or more groups for each year of age, there is sometimes random or alphabetical division, but often there is streaming by attainment. Children from middle-class homes have a greater verbal facility and altogether more advantages in expression and communication as judged by the school, over the child from a home minus books, conversation, and scholastic interest. At an early stage the home is the greatest influence and children who have lacked maternal care in infancy, followed by those with poor home conditions, do least well in the competition for A-stream places. Poorly clad and poorly cared for children find places in the lower streams when they are of limited ability more often than the less able child from a more caring home. They also find low stream places when their ability is of higher quality.

> The first unavoidable fact is that whatever else it does or could do, education is about equality. Education has always stood necessarily in close relation to class, status and power. In the past half century it has become part of the economic foundations of industrial society, a major avenue of social mobility and one of the principal agencies of social distribution. . . . There is clear evidence that social and educational conditions have a cumulative effect on measured ability. Slum children, in slum schools, whether or not they are born stupid, certainly become stupefied by their experiences.*

The teacher destined to teach the lower streams is often, in spite of the exhortations of educationalists, the new teacher or the less qualified teacher, so often the one who is likely to leave after a short period in keeping with the general rate of change and of marriage in the case of a young woman. The older teacher who has an allowance for special responsibility and is likely to stay for a length of time is much more likely to have the A-stream. Where, however, a special class is already recognized as a necessity, there is usually a special post for this teacher. Children are very sensitive to their lack of status. They have the new teacher, many changes of teacher, they put up perhaps with a condescending approach from many teachers who fail to meet them with understanding of their world. Sometimes in defence a low-streamed class develops a group awareness and a loyalty which gives security and some comfort. This is most often fostered by a caring, good teacher. Mostly the feelings of children in the lower streams are those of inferiority, disinterest, and aggression, whilst some parents wonder "What has gone wrong to make him into a B child".† Segregation in ability means segregation socially and perpetuation for the less able child of his failure. The fact that schools attempt to conceal their differentiation into streams

---

* A. Halsey, Education and equality, *New Society*, June 1965.

† Non-streaming in the junior school, P.S.W. Publications, *Forum*, 1966.

by devious devices, using P, Q, X, etc., for labels, indicates their partial understanding of the children's own feelings. For the children relegated from the age of 7 to these lower streams, the gap between them and the "able" children widens each year, and there is little hope that a C-child will change to a higher stream, particularly if he comes from a deprived home. Once allocated, children seem to take on characteristics of the group and those which are expected of them. Streaming therefore reinforces vigorously social selection.

Social discrepancy in life leads directly to discrepancies of educational progress and ability. The world is geared to the healthy, well-adjusted child. "The terrifying characteristic of British society is that many of those who are supposed to be inferior have been brainwashed into believing that they actually are."*

As we cannot but slowly right the social evils which drag down children, and as we cannot adequately safeguard them from the nature of their parents or from the hazards of this life, we must attempt to be sure that if possible we understand why a child is behaving at a subnormal level in school and that we give him every opportunity to use all his potential by extra generosity in provision, not by discarding and by thus promoting further subnormality.

It seems strange that so long after Dickens and Lord Shaftesbury, shocked as we all are at the thought of child cruelty, starvation, oppression, and corruption, we still have to become aware again of the world of the child. In our lack of imagination we still tolerate ignorance of the feelings of a child, the size of his feelings in his small world, and do not stop to think really what it is to be a child who is D or subnormal or to enter each day a school labelled ". . . E.S.N. School". Children must, of course, be aware that they are slower or less successful than others. We shall not be able to hide the fact behind disguised titles and class letters. Indeed, we shall not need to try to do so if we can, with sensitive understanding, bring self-respect and personal strength to these children.

* A. Wedgwood Benn, *Observer*, 5 January 1964.

There are, of course, children who for many reasons will need special education and who will always need special care in the community. The purpose of this latter discussion is to emphasize the part which the environment of the school may play in perpetuating the failure of less fortunate children, and to suggest that many children who still fail dismally and proceed without much progress in learning or in personal development to a doubtful place in the community, might be able in other circumstances, especially school circumstances, to take a responsible place in the adult world.

What factors eventually lead to a child being given a place in a special department or in a school for educationally subnormal children? The teacher certainly is the person who should best be able to estimate the potential and to understand the needs of a child who has been in her class for a term or more and who has been helped by records to compare her own observations with those of previous teachers. Children in large classes who sit quietly, causing no trouble, yet not participating fully or progressing with others, can be ignored by a busy non-observant teacher until they are hopelessly behind. Children who are bored, frustrated, or disturbed and cause disturbance are much more often referred by a class teacher for examination, and many children who are given places in special schools have been difficult children, behaving in a disturbing way in the ordinary class.

In many areas the heads and teachers in the schools do have great influence in determining which children go to special schools. We have discussed already the tendencies of teachers to confuse children's appearance and social background with ability. True as this is, the teacher is still the best judge of a child's need for special education.

The intelligence quotient is not a fundamental measure of intelligence, and by itself is of little importance. "The millions of man hours devoted to preparing, administering, scoring and interpreting mental measurements have yielded a tiny dust heap of knowledge about language, thought, growth and meaning."*

* G. D. Stoddard, *The Meaning of Intelligence*, p. 26.

Children who are failing in their school tasks, who are disturbed and emotionally starved, often suffer further under testing, and for them intelligence tests are unreliable. The test does not, particularly for these children, give a valid indication of ability. Such tests may indicate a greater or lesser intellectual efficiency at the time of testing, but do not really give a true idea of potential.

> It is one thing to use the tests positively to identify children with a potentiality a good deal higher than their education attainments suggest. It is quite another matter to use them negatively to "prove" that low scoring children can never be expected to achieve a normal level of education, and so to justify their teacher's neglect. The inevitable unreliability of all mental and educational tests, together with the impossibility of constructing pure tests of intelligence mean that a low score may give a totally false impression of a particular child's potentiality. There is a very simple safeguard against such errors . . . a high score on an intelligence test is always of significance, to the teacher, a low score might be.*

What it is necessary to stress is that tests of any kind for the apparently less able child are apt to be misleading, and although it may be necessary for some teachers to ascertain levels of achievement by tests, they should be acutely aware of the discrepancy in results, influenced as they are by the emotional climate surrounding a child at the time of testing, and of the impossibility of making a test valid for children whose difficulties and backgrounds have such individual stresses. Educational assessment must be linked with the programme which is in progress at the time, in the classroom.

All conditions of endowment, experience, home, and school contribute to the factors which result in the child being given a place in the special class, department, or school for the educationally subnormal. These are the children who make up the communities with which I am concerned. It would seem that even with all the possibilities of misjudgement which exist, on the whole children in these classes and departments are those who really need special help and attention for many reasons. It is this great variety of disability and maladjustment that makes it

* Stephen Wiseman, In defence of intelligence tests, *New Society*, May 1964.

so important that a teacher knows the children as well and as sympathetically as is possible, that a teacher remains with his class for a year or more during a child's life in a particular school, that the classes and groupings are small enough for a teacher to be able to know them well, and that materials and conditions are generously enough supplied so that the children's individual needs may be met.

In some areas it is almost an unknown event for a child to return from a special to the ordinary school. There seems to be the same inflexibility which exists in the case of streaming in some primary schools, which means that once a child has been given a place in a special school it is not likely that he will return. There are many reasons for this. Heads say often when asked about the return of pupils to the secondary school that they would be fearful lest the social adjustment and progress in personal security made were not sufficiently strong and integrated to make such readjustment possible. Children do become secure and happy in special schools, they grow in self-esteem and positiveness, and one can sympathize with the head's point of view. The general public still does not understand sympathetically and intelligently the handicap which makes a child slower or mentally less able, or more insecure and unstable than his fellows. We still meet the stigma of the "daft school" or "the loonies". Parents are ashamed until they fully appreciate the advantages to be gained for their children. Special classes in the ordinary school suffer more from their internal environment. They are "special" in a smaller world, their superior being around them continually. The special class may have more child-centred education, a room which looks more exciting, more like a workshop, but theirs is a different existence. The others sit, they "learn", and may look with disdain at the "baby" work going on in the special class. It will take a revolution in secondary teaching, long overdue, to bring it nearer to the progressive teaching which sometimes goes on in a special class, and to bridge this gap.

One wonders if the quality of teaching in our special classes and schools can be good enough to redress the balance of the scorn and ridicule which exist to torment the child and the parents of children in the special school or department.

It is obvious that one cannot generalize about the nature of these children. There is, as with all children, no description which will fit more than a single child. There is danger that one does receive a general impression and tends to label these children with characteristics which become reinforced by the climate of the school or class. All these children have learning difficulties, in varying areas and degrees, for many different reasons. Many are unstable and there is an atmosphere affected by changing mood, changing of friends, and temper tantrums, and sometimes there is an air of tension which forebodes unusual behaviour.

Many are rigid in attitude and are unable to adapt to new situations, so that a change in routine must be taken more slowly and steadily than one would in a normal school. There is a more ready acceptance of concrete thinking than of concepts, so that behaviour, arrangements, and censorship have to be explained in a way which the children can imagine and understand. For inst-ance, a headmaster attempted to help a boy towards accepted sexual behaviour in his senior school by placing before him the concrete facts of the cost in money to him of the baby, which might be the consequence of his behaviour. One may approve or disapprove of his method and his explanation, but can appre-ciate the need he felt to make the boy understand in concrete terms and ones which he could feel deeply because he cared about money.

Many children are late to mature physically, socially, and emotionally, or in one or two of these ways, and because this is a characteristic of a large number of these children, they must be specially safeguarded and helped towards self-dependence and social competence.

There is also a preponderance of lack of persistence. It is often difficult for them to concentrate for a normal span of attention for their age. They are inhibited by past experience of failure and lack of understanding in a learning situation. There are many who withdraw, some who have fear in their whole attitude and reflected in their eyes. Such fear may be the overflow of real physical fear, but it is more often a fear of the world of teachers, parents, other adults and children, surrounding their school life. There is a shrinking from challenges and a lack of inner motivation, independent energy and confidence. This has to grow slowly and steadily. They tend therefore to imitate and to offer little original thought, even if they are capable of doing so.

Each one of these children is a personality, individual in ability and in failure, and in assessing some of the main characteristics of children in schools for the so-called educationally subnormal one is by no means describing an individual child. One of the biggest dangers is that children in such a community are expected to conform to a pattern such as is described by a headmaster or educationalist when talking of these children. If the expectation is for limitation in all directions, it is no wonder that the children appear to become of like subnormality, eased and sedated by the security of life in the special school or department.

CHAPTER 6

MEASUREMENT

LET US consider for a moment some ways in which people find amusement and through which some reach fame. There are beauty contests ranging from "Miss Dairymaid" to "Miss World". Judges attempt to pick a winner, to put in order the attributes of physique which are mainly God-given and to measure that visible evidence of poise and inner harmony that gives from within beauty to a person's body. Others compete in breaking-up pianos, eating pies, drinking beer, or in long-playing drum sessions.

One gets nearer to understanding the reason for competition when mechanics compete in stripping down cars, farmers in sheep shearing or ploughing. The world cup final emptied the streets on a Saturday afternoon. Wimbledon and the Olympic games are similarly followed with eager attention, and it is a comparatively rare person who scorns any interest in national or international athletic or games competitions.

Lovers of music listen eagerly for results of competitions to find and reward the best young violinist or pianist of the year, artists have pictures hung at the Royal Academy; Oscars are presented to film stars.

There is in human nature an appetite for competition. Society uses this way to give appreciation and opportunity to its members, to establish and express loyalties and a sense of belonging. So surely is competition accepted and established that the commercial world uses it for its own ends without question of the need to prepare society for it. It needs no introduction.

What of competition and of the instruments of measurement in education? Competition comes naturally in play. Children race up the street, collect more marbles, play ludo and "dare" more than their friends. We win or lose. There is a place for the urge to higher standards set by competitors and for the fight to win. How hard it is for some runners and swimmers to race against a stop-watch without the incentive of the other person pounding along in front or behind. There is a place for reward for activity well done, for striving, for care and preparation, and for the fullest use of ability. The reward is, however, present in any case. It is in the triumph, happiness, and deep satisfaction of doing one's utmost, or achievement within oneself.

The reason for this chapter is my growing fear of measurement brought about by educational trends, trends which loom larger even as concepts of opportunity for all, comprehensive education, and abolition of the most doubtful sorting agent, the 11-plus, are upon us.

Education needs research into ways and means, results, and possibilities. We must not, of course, depend only upon our observations and intuitive knowledge of children, our faith in them, and our belief in ourselves, although we shall not proceed far without these; but we must consider the dangers of attempting to come to conclusions which, too firmly established, without the proof which only time and much observation can give, might set back the progress of education for years as the faith given to the intelligence quotient may have done. We must look at the reasons why we wish to make certain measurements, what we are measuring, and how valid the answers are likely to be, for whom and for how long. Measurement as an instrument of evaluation of the needs of children and of the success of our communication, to help us to judge changes and to make decisions about our teaching, is essential, but the usual methods of testing are limited tools, too global in approach, and they interfere with rather than enhance learning, especially for the less successful child.

Why do many teachers measure even beyond the amount

required by the authority concerned? Does testing make the teacher more secure, more confident that he is imparting knowledge, reassured that the job is being done? Examinations might spur on the pupils to greater effort, making them get down to it. Does he not trust his own ability to interest and instil a liking for learning? Testing keeps the class very quiet; it uses time in what looks like a proper way, it leads to peace and industry. Very neat and tidy is the day of examination papers, time setting, paper clips, and a consequent pile of visible results of a teacher's effort. Some teachers and many head teachers like to have many lists. Lists "button up" the loose ends, things are rounded, neat, tidy, and in hand. Children certainly resent it if they are left out of an examination pattern in a school. We have succeeded in establishing for them the importance of examinations as a status symbol.

I remember in a London County Council school standing round the edge of the classroom at the end of the term in order of merit, when the long strips of paper which bore the examination results in order had all emerged. This order was used to establish desk positions for the next term, until the next examinations, when there was a remote chance of there being a desk shuffle. We still have class order in reports. What does it really mean in terms of an individual?

Often the child who continually succeeds and "sits high" and firmly, can treat it rather like a game, the score is to be as high as possible; examination papers are like party games or crossword puzzles—a change from the routine of lessons. If he is not good at recapitulation under stress, however, or has no mind for facts, it will not be a game. Those friends of mine who stood regularly at the far, lowest end of the room and then sat on the far side at the back each term, did not find it game-like, even if to cover their shame they acted like clowns, wallowing in their foolishness. For the succeeding child examinations might be an incentive, but for the less successful, measuring in "order of merit" against one's fellows is not very helpful.

If then, considering the seriousness of the implications for those who do not ever do well, we accept that some examining is necessary in school to indicate the needs of a child further, then could we see that examinations and tests applied are really necessary and profitable, and perhaps more important, that we leave for all children and students some things which are not measurable in examination terms, things which are done because they are joyous, through which a child can really play again, which bring feelings of satisfaction rather than those of success, which he does for reasons deeper than measurement? I am speaking of painting, making things, singing, and all kinds of music making and the enjoyment of music, movement, drama and dance, and writing, the purpose of which is to express ideas; I mean, in fact, all those languages through which a child comes to communicate his feelings, thoughts, ideas, and needs.

Let us look at the sense and nonsense of measuring. Do testing and examining take up valuable teaching time which they do not merit? Do they also take the time of a teacher who marks all the resulting papers, tediously spending hours in repetitive work when he might be enriching himself for the task in hand, or refreshing himself and becoming a more creative person?

Whilst teachers are measuring the mechanics of reading, could they not be getting on with the help so urgently needed by the non-readers and poor readers? One is reminded of the Scottish school where, unable to keep up with the daily reading session, a child resorted to rote learning. Failure accompanied by misery, sickness, and bed wetting resulted because this kind of testing replaced the help he needed; drudgery and fear replaced effort. It is true that most teachers who hear children read have only the desire to help the individual child, and most often this kind of fear is not incurred. On the contrary, it is for most children the rare occasion when they receive individual help. The difficulties arise because teachers giving such attention to a single child have so many other children waiting for their turn, and it is still an uncommon situation when a teacher has help with reading where there are many children whose reading ability is backward. If a certain remedial teacher in a secondary school did as she was advised by her inspector and heard every child read every day, she would never give her children any of her attention in any other way, and she is a person who believes that her girls need incentive to encourage them to read.

Reading readiness is not measurable. It is a complex factor of richness of environment and experience. Any material urging mothers to teach their babies to read may be doing children a serious disservice. Already a parent says with alarm in her voice, "He cannot read, he is 6". A teacher says, "He cannot read, and soon he will go to the junior school". Now we have the possibility of parents saying, "He is 3 and he cannot read". What is this ability to read about which we are so anxious? It is a recognition of shapes of letters, then of words which will only with living in the world of language and things become understanding and communication. "What price in terms of failure and misery are we willing to pay for early achievement of school learning?"*

A head of a department in a school writes:

> In an academic year of forty weeks can the interruption of normal teaching for examinations and the correction of papers once or even twice, be justified? In order that reports may be completed before the holidays examinations frequently take place at least three weeks before the end of term and serious work is seldom assumed afterwards. If examinations are held twice yearly the loss of time may be five or six weeks, at least one-eighth of the school year. If this loss of teaching time is to be justified, those who insist on examinations for junior forms must demonstrate their value in precise educational terms.
>
> The traditional arguments in favour of these examinations appear to be that they ensure that work is learnt thoroughly, that work in the summer term is purposive, that there is thorough revision and that pupils shou d learn to work under examination conditions. To accept these arguments is to indict the whole teaching profession, for the inference is that we are unable to provide reasonable incentives to learning. How useful is a week's special revision before an examination covering a whole year's work? If such revision is needed what may we think of the months of work which preceded it? It is not surprising to find that where an examination is given to the least able, sympathetic teachers select topics for revision so that pupils are prepared and know what to expect on the papers which follow.
>
> A yearly or half-yearly assessment is essential for staff and for parents. How is it to be made without an examination? After marking an examination script, a good teacher will know nothing about a pupil which was not

---

* H. Lytton, How soon should children read?, *New Society*, July 1966.

obvious before. Clearly all depends upon effective teaching and careful recording of progress, and if these are lacking can one really believe that the deficiencies will be corrected by an annual examination? A school with poor teachers will remain poor whether or not there are examinations.*

There is limited feed-back from examinations to the pupils. Once the marks are given there is little motivation for the less successful examinee to find out about things that he did not know and often he is hesitant to display once again his ignorance. An examination mostly tests whether he does or does not know, but is care taken to put right his lack of knowledge or particular ability?

Two books published by Clifford Allen, *Passing School Examinations* and *Passing Examinations*, make quite clear the level at which the author places the examination. Children are rated little higher than performers of examination tricks.

If one watches circus animals performing it will be seen that the trainer always gives the animal a piece of meat or some other food when it has successfully accomplished a trick. A child can be conditioned just as easily as animals, but the tragedy is that nobody has the patience to try with small children.†

It is true that few educationalists would take this author seriously in his advice to parents, but it has nevertheless reached published form and without doubt, some parents will.

Lord David Cecil, looking at higher education, used the title *Examinations, the end of Education?* He writes:

Obsession with examination results has infected all England [and concludes] The odd thing is that this trend is against the modern trend of educational theory which is opposed to trial by examination. We are always hearing of the harm done by the 11+ examination, of the dreadful way it strains a child's nerves and weakens his natural interests. But the same thing is true of examinations at 15+, and 18+, and 21+. It is time educationalists began campaigning against them.‡

---

* Letter to *The Times Educational Supplement*, 22 July 1966. The writer of this letter preferred to remain anonymous.

† Clifford Allen, *Passing School Examinations*, p. 86.

‡ Reported from *Venture*, the magazine of Leicester College of Education, where it was reprinted with permission from Heinemann and the *Daily Telegraph*.

We must know, of course, in a subject where it can be ascertained, if a child has reached this or that understanding which is a prerequisite for further progress, but surely so much testing is not necessary for a teacher to do this. One comes across children in a classroom, children who have their task in number all right or all wrong, consistently, indicating especially in the latter case, that no amount of testing has given sufficient information to that teacher and that observation of this child's attempts to work would be helpful.

Examinations become a status symbol. The number of C.S.E. or G.C.E. passes stands now in the senior school as did the number of scholarships gained to the grammar school in the primary department. Children may be the least important factors. Some are entered for examination as one might buy another six balls at a coconut shy. "C.S.E. or G.C.E. ?" "Enter both and see what happens." Examinations loom large in the mind of most teachers. G.C.E. and C.S.E. groups become most important in a school where there are large groups of children who are not succeeding with the beginnings of literacy. How is it that the gaining of two or three O-level passes for five or six boys can take such a major part of staff effort in a school whilst a group of children receive insufficient individual attention to lift them for a while from their bored inadequacy?

Large sums of money are spent on equipment for science and other academic work for very few pupils in a particular secondary school, whilst the majority of pupils, and especially the least able, have a minimal share of available finance for special literature and materials.

Members of a school staff, especially heads of subject departments, show often little understanding of the least able children, so that unless the latter are protected by a special teacher who really understands them, they are likely to flounder disastrously when put into the school pattern of examinations.

What does it all mean? I quote from an article headed, "Mysteries of Aesthetics":

The twenty institute members completed Penrose form manipulation tests, EPI (personality) tests, intelligence tests and most important, a test to examine an hypothesis of George D. Birkhoff, an American mathematician, expounded in his book *Aesthetic Measure*. Orderly and disorderly simple and complex polygons were projected on a screen in rapid series and were rated by the subjects on an eight point scale.

Birkhoff's hypothesis states that aesthetic worth or measure (M) is related to the order (O) and complexity (C) of an object. In the test, complexity is related to the number of sides of the polygons and order to such factors as symmetry and equilibrium. The aim, according to Birkhoff, is: "Within each class of aesthetic objects, to define the order and complexity so that their ratio $M = O \div C$ yields the aesthetic measure of any object of the class."

This formula hasn't gone unchallenged. In his essay "The Psychology of Aesthetics", Eysenck argues that a long series of experiments have led him to the conclusion that Birkhoff's formula is wrong, and that the correct one is $M = O \times C$. In other words the most preferred kind of object is that with both a high degree of order and of complexity.

The whole operation sounds complex, but that hasn't deterred about 2000 pre-diploma art students and 2000 non-art students in Britain from already being tested in a similar fashion. The vast amount of data emerging from these tests will need time and a computer. Staffs at some art schools have been hostile to the tests on the traditional grounds that the essential elements, if any, of aesthetic experience are unquantifiable. But they have later come round to using the tests for student selection. Such is the prestige of science in an age when art school prospectuses speak of "design science" and "design axiomatics".*

It is relevant here to talk of the Bachelor of Education degree. Important as it is that the student educated for three years to become a teacher should receive the status and recognition as a graduate, if his work reaches this standard, enormous harm may come to the children as a result. Patterns of assessment which have been operating for years now are displaced by more limiting written examinations. Worse, within the college of education comes an attitude of measurement which may override considerations of richness of personality, involvement with the needs of children, and the whole range of qualities and learning which make a caring, lively teacher.

This effort to "get into" the B.Ed. at all costs and to deal with the necessary consequences afterwards does not bode well for children, particularly for those who need teachers who care,

* 'Mysteries of aesthetics', report of an experiment in psychological aesthetics, *New Society*, July 1966.

understand unusually well and have insight into the growth of people as well as the knowledge of history, mathematics, or educational theory to write on paper. There is here, however, a great opportunity for the enrichment of education through deepened study and thoroughness made possible by extra time, if the needs of children can be maintained as the primary factor in the task of educating teachers of higher quality.

At the same time there is the race by teachers into colleges of education, and inside these colleges, as in schools, the race for promotion. How do we measure teachers and lecturers, to say who is to have an allowance, a senior, or a principal lecturership?

One of the areas of education which exhibits disturbing tendencies is physical education. It is not always easy for physical education to find itself recognized as being academically respectable. In fact physical education, especially on the women's side, has a magnificent record for service, child awareness, and educational involvement, and in pursuing values which are unique to this subject there is no need for shame or subterfuge. Is there not far too great an accent on measuring human physiques and physical development at the expense of that which concerns physical well-being and growth of children's personalities?

One cannot measure a child and certainly one cannot measure expressive activity. How does one mark a piece of writing when one has asked for "creation", "freedom", and "communication"? How does one mark a child's painting, his acting or dancing? Who are we to judge and why should we need to try?

Dance teachers feel the need to become "respectable", too, and even here, where the child can be himself most fully, there is dange of the pressure of notation and even of the language of movement itself taking precedence over the needs of the child to use such language to communicate. We could kill the spontaneity, joy, and satisfying positiveness of dance by giving an accent upon notation symbols too early or upon intricate language analysis. We could destroy by the very understanding which makes the art live, just as physical education is in some danger of becoming joyless and playless. We distrust pleasure; we think it trivial. We dare not allow it to be free.

How can one measure a teacher? What does a B mean under teaching on a certificate? There are some things which are so involved with qualities, with untidy things like sensitivity, awareness, sympathy, vitality, generosity, inner harmony, and the blending of knowledge and understanding, that measurement can be at best meaningless. There are enough warring factors which fight in the lives of children without their being involved with the status of their teacher.

> Education should be primarily addressed to the "not-self".
>
> When harmony has been established with this massive silent partner, the powers of the self are quickened in an amazing way.
>
> I relax with the artist as guide, in order to increase the efficiency of this understanding and use.*

Are the least able children to be submerged in our new educational world under the weight of the examination stress, beneath the race for status and promotion and the short-sightedness of those who think that only measured things are "done"?

* J. N. Todd (Ed.), *Arts, Artists and Thinkers*, p. 326.

CHAPTER 7

SCHOOL-LEAVERS

In a previous chapter dealing with behaviour problems I made the observation that in most residential schools, and indeed in most day special schools for educationally subnormal children, problems of bad behaviour were not disturbing the equilibrium of the community. In most schools there was greater quiet and order than one finds in the ordinary secondary modern, comprehensive, or even grammar school. The schools had, of course, smaller numbers, but the sense of peace reigning was on the whole attributable to the fact that heads and teachers in these schools knew the necessity for security of pattern, for a routine surrounding such children with safety and calm, making it possible for them to learn to the best of their ability. Sometimes the atmosphere seemed excessively calm, almost "drugged".

Such an atmosphere may be right for most of the children and it certainly helps the staff to fulfil their teaching tasks and to live in the community with less strain, but one wonders how the transition from this atmosphere to the outside world is to be effected safely for these children. There might be a move from the country mansion to a home in a crowded city or a farm cottage, from extreme cleanliness to some measure of squalor, from order and time-table throughout the day to the rush and disorder of life, from the protection of housemother and teachers in a children's community to the harsh, materialistic, real world.

How great a shock is this going to be? I know that in many cases there are hostels for these children. He or she is 16, one year older than the leaver from the ordinary school. How much less mature, however, can these young people be? There are after-care schemes and these are growing. When, however, one considers the huge gap between the community of the special school and the factory floor or workshop and all the responsibilities which life in the outside world brings, it is obvious that however the transition is eased, much effort must be made to strengthen the personality and to secure standards and habits so that these young people may stand more chance of adjustment.

Many schools do make great efforts to effect the transition gradually during the last years. Boys and girls are sent on shopping expeditions, or travel tasks, and are out doing work for a part of the week. Teachers are not unaware of the difficulties. Indeed, I have heard teachers of educationally subnormal children say that the one thing which concerned them was that the children should be able to cope with life when they left school.

It would appear to be the time of greatest danger for these young people. There would seem to be for some an inevitable pathway to delinquency. For the senior girl, needing as she does so often affection and acceptance, immature in personality, yet mature in body, there is the greatest danger.

This aspect must be kept in mind when later we discuss how we should teach these children. The only real way to protect them is to make them personally capable of taking their place in a community. This cannot always be done, but we can work towards it, hoping that the after-care services which must be provided will bridge the gap.

Let us look more carefully at the transitional shock for the girl or boy from a special department or school.

The transfer from school to work, college, or university, is in any case a crucial one. The transition becomes greater as one descends the scale of academic attainment. For the intending graduate there is still to some extent the ordered world of academic study, refectory meals, tradition, and some guidance from adults who stand for things which are not immediately material. For the young person from a secondary modern school there is most often the rough transit into manual employment. This means much longer hours than at school, getting off in the rush of the morning without the aid of the school bus; it often means poor working conditions and hard physical work which a growing young person can find taxing. They are the newest comers, the easiest scapegoats for some older workers. In some smaller firms conditions of work can be very poor, supervision inadequate, and protection by factory laws and union rights less likely.

A young person may become bored with monotonous work, fatigued by heat and noise, apathetic, and resentful. Grumbling may be already existing so he or she joins in. It is the thing to do and goes on in the toilets, at the tea break—maybe all the time. There is in such a community a striving to establish superiority, and the new youngsters are the victims of others' superiority drives. There may be arguments and petty rows, scandals, threats, and fights. There may be little incentive for a worker to give effort, and the attitude of disdain and boredom is easily caught and established.

This kind of transfer can bring breakdown at all levels. A boy or girl is "on his or her own" in a harsh, rushing world where good times, clothes, "things", and sex are important, where honesty and human sympathy appear to be unheeded.

What then are the counteracting influences which may help? First it must be said that many industrial concerns are careful for the welfare of their employees. Not only do they cater for their recreation, as in large factories such as Cadbury Bros. Ltd., but they appoint and train workers carefully and have staff in charge of personnel who really have understanding, intelligence, and integrity, often learned on the factory floor, through years of contact with fellow workers. Older workers, too, are not always uncaring, and some fortunate entrants come into contact with kind, experienced people who try to act as parent substitutes. The Youth Employment Service receives much criticism, but many youth employment officers take trouble and care, but find the task difficult if contact is not made possible, and young people tend to avoid guidance of this kind once they have left school, or do not know that it is available for them. Youth employment officers have the task of helping to place pupils, and as one employer pointed out, the officer would not jeopardize placing his brighter pupils by sending inadequate applicants. The same employer, an intelligent, socially conscientious person, pointed out that her job was to make the firm pay, not to do social service.

Schools, too, most often try to maintain contact, but this is a link which the least adequate children most often wish to break. Youth service does not touch enough of these young people. The coffee bar is less demanding and less structured, the dance hall more sophisticated. Young people feel that they are being patronized by youth and church club organizations. Is it possible that coffee-bar proprietors and publicans could come to care?

Home should, of course, provide the most secure buffer for the world of the factory, but in many cases this is not so. In the case of the young person most severely in need it is certainly not so.

The ultimate protection is the strength and integrity in a person built up from childhood, his social awareness, and his ability to look around for opportunity for leisure which is rewarding, and to stand firm for those things which he sees to be right and good. This is perhaps an idealistic approach condemnable in this present day for its optimism. For our educationally subnormal leavers all difficulties are greater because of their lesser maturity, less resistance to applied pressures, often less adequate home backgrounds, and because for them education has been in the first place an area of failure and then one where special attention, care, and protection have been given.

I endeavoured to obtain factual information about work taken by these school-leavers and their progress in early working years. This information could not often be gained from the schools who maintain on the whole limited contact with pupils. Factories, such as the British United Shoe Machinery Co., Cadbury Bros. Ltd., Corah's, and Symingtons, were very willing to discuss the problem and to show me their training schemes in action. There are many firms, such as the British Shoe Machinery Co., Leicester, where, although formerly only having employed as apprentices grammar school boys, they now accept C-stream secondary modern school boys, have few places for the less able except as cleaners, tidyers, and messengers. One can be sure that where a less able young person acquires a position in one of these reputed industries, they receive care and security, if not advancement materially, but young people even of limited intelligence do not accept this kind of work as their job in life or are not allowed to do so by more ambitious parents.

In many reputable factories there is a detailed interview, often a medical check, subsequent care, and still for the employers some measure of choice of employee. This does not necessarily rule out the possibility of the educationally subnormal leaver gaining entry, although the personnel officer of one large concern who told me that they took very little notice of school reports but relied upon their own impression and skill in observing, expressed some horror that they might have taken somebody from a special school. The educationally subnormal pupil leaves school often well mannered, well spoken, and charming, and might well in many cases give a better impression at an interview than a more aggressive, rougher mannered secondary modern pupil. Once in, however, the problem of speed and manual dexterity may become a difficulty. Repetitive jobs can necessitate also that the worker "knows" the machine. Team work can present difficulties because a slower member of a team can become a liability in piece-work and therefore unpopular and a scapegoat for ill feeling.

Nevertheless, it would be very good if industries with a structure which ensures personal care, cleanliness, medical, and educational provision and facilities for leisure could take a proportion of educationally subnormal school-leavers. In such an atmosphere many would become very good workers, and would have every chance of leading steady adult lives with purpose and happiness.

There is evidence that success in employment is not noticeably linked for these children with ability in classroom subjects. Failure in employment is most often from the employers' point of view due to slowness, unreliability exhibited in absence for minor reasons, cessation of work when unsupervised, difficulty in communication, resentment of criticism, and limited co-operation.

Social immaturity is a very important factor. The less able children often find mixing difficult, but obviously some gain ground very markedly. "Social adjustment after leaving school and I.Q. (some years earlier) show virtually no correlation."*

Sometimes they have not realized their own limited potential and over-ambition supported by parents has been a problem. Educationally subnormal girl leavers are sometimes kept at home as housekeepers even when the mother has to go out to work. Such a girl goes on being protected but has little chance of social development. Many change jobs frequently; they are unstable, wanting change to something different, not really making friends or settling into a pattern of life.

It is, of course, impossible to generalize. So much depends upon the person and his difficulties. A young person who is still emotionally disturbed is unlikely to acquire stability in a working situation. The home is very important and might make all the difference between a worker who persists and settles and one who joins the ranks of the changers from job to job, the unsettled, the social liability.

Nevertheless, there is no doubt that in spite of the difficulties there are a large number of these children who, when they have left school behind, merge into the working world and become ordinary people who in time live down the fact that they were in a special school or department, and perhaps because of the special care and training lead satisfactory lives. The transition to work is hard for these people, and the ultimate life product in human terms is likely to be less adequate, the implication being that there may well be perpetuation in the next generation through deprived home life, of the inadequacy with which we have endeavoured to deal in education.

It is necessary to add to this pessimistic note by looking at the immediate future in industry. What do the less able people face as speed and accuracy become more important? "We are told

* *Youth Employment*, vol. 14, no. 2, winter, 1961–62, p. 19.

that automation leads to a higher proportion of semi-skilled jobs which demand proper training."*

How fast are changes coming and how often will a worker have to readjust? Is the development of more sophisticated methods to mean less employment for the unskilled and less able teenager? "Will increasing automation mean that in the long run fewer skills will be needed for the many and higher skills for the minority?"†

Industry is looking for a better educated girl and boy which bode ill for the educationally handicapped. In America there is awareness of the necessity made by widespread automation to give urgency to the need for improving education. If automation is to necessitate a smaller, younger, more flexible labour force, the need for educational research into the problems of educating our less able pupils for living is even more urgent than before.

Associated is the problem of leisure, both immediate, as the young worker is faced with mass media and with time on his hands, and later as more time becomes available. Most of these people will have a job which is apart from their leisure. Good leisure time can only result from a working life which engenders self-respect. In educating these children, reading and writing are only a small part, even though in a literate community, an important part.

It is with these problems in mind that the teaching of educationally subnormal pupils must be considered. Much thought about school learning techniques does not reach the future for these young people. There are almost insuperable problems here, and this book only looks at an area of education and experience within which there lies great potential for personal development—that of the expressive arts.

* The choice of a career, *The Times Educational Supplement*, July 1965.
† Working men in an age of automation, *The Times Educational Supplement*, February 1965.

CHAPTER 8

THE LANGUAGE OF WORDS—
A MAJOR PROBLEM

> Man clings to language as tightly as the oyster to his shell. What more
> terrifying thing could the witches in Macbeth be doing than "a deed with-
> out a name". People feel a real unease and separation when confronted
> by the nameless, and it is perfectly understandable that the first man set
> down in the centre of the first landscape applied himself at once to re-
> deeming it from anonymity.*

This chapter contributes both to the discussion of the problem
being considered and to the alleviation of the problem. The
language of words is for these children a major difficulty in
communication, but talking and being with conversation are
extremely important avenues whereby they may share experiences
and become socially competent.

> Yet of course, the highly centralized, bureaucratized and industrialized
> communities of the modern world, with their characteristic high degree
> of urbanization involve a communication system for which literacy con-
> stitutes a basic necessity.†

The advance of the necessity for literacy has been in line with
economic development, with compulsory schooling, and increasingly as the acquisition of education is related to social status.
These skills become important for the increasing numbers of
people who explore legacies in books and for those who develop
the sophisticated art of writing. The advent of increasing leisure
time makes it important that the written works are available to as

* Quoted from F. Ponge by R. Wilber in *Poetry and the Landscape* and included
in G. Kepes, *The New Landscape in Arts and Science*, p. 86.

† G. H. Bantock, reviewing *English for the Rejected* by D. Holbrook in *Education
for Teaching*, November 1964.

many as possible. The desirability of an informed community makes fluent reading imperative if one considers that education can ultimately inculcate discrimination and criticism of that which is written.

Many adults leave reading, except for pictorial papers and magazines, behind them upon leaving school. Few write more than the occasional letter. Yet the stigma of being unable to read and write adequately, if discovered, is a severe one. This is marked for the child who does not acquire these skills at a relatively "normal age", whatever that might be educationally at the time. The village headmistress who was about to retire, when questioned by an education officer about the reading ability of the children in her class, drew herself up to her fullest height and replied indignantly, "None of my children leaves me at seven still unable to read". Parents have caught this accent and one hears often, "Can he read yet?" from one mother to another. There was a period, in infant education especially, when teachers were persuaded that reading readiness was a stage of development which should not be anticipated, but many teachers did not allow this to be so, feeling a guilt which belied their own philosophy, and educationalists, whilst expounding progressive theories to students and teachers, make certain that their own children are able to read as early as possible.

Reading and writing, however, important as they are, must be for the majority of people the lesser tools of communication. Education has in its urge to teach, and at all costs to teach a child to read, write, and deal with number, but it often neglected the predominant tool—that of speech. We have realized that in the acquisition of foreign language, speech is fundamental and must precede and be concurrent with the written word, but it has taken longer for teachers to become aware of the necessity to develop in children the art of fluent speech.

Speech grows from the individual exploring and imitating of sounds to become the instrument of social intercourse, our main means of communication, engendering human contact which feeds in more language.

A child, delighting in sound plays with words. "This is my juggen-jugger" and "This is my hoen-digger". If speech goes on around him he imitates and assimilates words rapidly. A normal environment is rich with speech from fond and admiring adults, the world is lively with sound, and with such encouragement the spoken language develops easily and naturally. "Progress in mastery of language is not a matter of simple instruction and willing response, but very largely one of natural development, through the appearance of fresh insights."*

Language and thought develop inseparably. As a child finds fresh experience and comes to feel and think, as feelings are nourished and language develops, he grows in his power to hold ideas. Through language he comes to control his feelings, and with response to words his interests become pursuable. There must be meaningfulness where words are concerned, concrete experience with words, communication with people who respond visibly and verbally, more action, and the developing ability to assemble words into communicating form.

Judgement and categorization of words and things come about with some difficulty for many of the children with whom we are at this moment concerned, and they need help to experience them practically alongside word usage. They need guidance so that they may have experiences which they may not themselves seek, so that their language may stand a chance of meaningful expansion and development. There needs to be "over-information", "over-experience", and strengthening of the perception and feeling beyond that which one would imagine to be necessary. We need also to strengthen our own feeling capacities and imaginative quality to make us fitted for such "over-experience".

Language is necessary for a person to comprehend life, to form concepts, and judgements. These children are held back from life by lack of language, so that as we feed the language of the environment itself, of sound, shape, movement, and interaction, we must feed the language of words which bring about thought, understanding, and more words. "Words play a central part,

* A. F. Watts, *The Language and Mental Development of Children*, p. 244.

not only in the development of thought but in the historical growth of consciousness as a whole. A word is a microcosm of human consciousness."*

A word without meaning is nothing and will not last or serve a useful purpose, and a thought which has not words available is intangible. "I wanted to utter a word, but that word I cannot remember, and the bodiless thought will now return to the place of shadows."†

A child obviously goes through a stage of pre-intellectual speech and of thinking before speech has become adequately available, but the connection grows until the two are bound and the meaning of words is such a unity of thinking and speaking that it is most often not possible to say where the initiative arises. Thought is embodied in speech, and words acquire meaning. We cannot and need not argue here about the preciseness of the development of speech and thought for a child, whether language is fitted on to thought, and how much language contributes to the formation of concepts. It is certain that sensory and motor activities help a child enormously to recognize and classify, and that language offers a frame of reference for storage and retrieval.

One might ask why the child who fails in school apparently learns so much and understands and retains so little. Behind all this lies the child himself, his volitional and affective life and his maturity. Words are for living, for interaction between people which takes away fear. We see in the deaf child the effect of language impairment, the poverty of reasoning power, of comprehension, recall, and cognition. Evidence is ample of the influence of language acquisition upon learning and understanding. So often for the less able child there is a vicious circle, of deprivation of environment and language impoverishment, and the developing inability to comprehend. Development of language is a social process and thought is the life of language.

We must find ways of developing language confidence and of

* L. S. Vygotsky, *Thought and Language*, p. 153.
† *Ibid.*, p. 509.

stimulating the use of words, with patience, through the stages of lack of coherence, of necessary repetition to the finding of logical relationships and understanding. A teacher must be liaison between non-discussive talkers in a group, until the art of communication and of conversation develops. Talking and conversation, listening and contributing, are ever-necessary for these particular children. "The man that says nothing is a disquieting and uncanny creature."*

Talking must be the main means of communication in school for these children, yet even in their educational programme one finds often an accent upon the struggle to read and write and to listen. In infant and in other lively primary schools, and sometimes in the upper forms of senior schools, one can hear discussion, children recounting to others and to the teacher their experiences and ideas, and an interchange of talk and response. I recently heard a discussion by juniors about books they had read. This discussion took place whilst the children were engaged in art and craft work. The situation was a right one, the children confident; it was as one would have thought a most natural occasion, yet so unusual was the fluency that one found oneself startled and disbelieving.

The denial of opportunity for speech has serious developmental consequences, far beyond those relating to lack of reading and writing experience. Luria and Yudovic, in their work with backward twins, found that the degree of lack of mental development was directly related to the degree of lack of speech development.†

The fluent use of speech, besides being a major factor in the development of a communicating person, feeds into the desire and ability to use words in writing and to discover words in books. The interest in language, its excitement for its own sake and for that which it contains, is to be sponsored through the spoken word, through stories told, poetry read, and through conversation.

* O. Jesperson, *Mankind, Nation and Individual*, p. 9.
† A. R. Luria and I. I. Yudovic, *Speech and Development of Mental Processes in the Child.*

Yet, even in this enlightened day teachers are habitual inhibitors of talk. To talk in class is often to earn displeasure, even punishment. Every teacher experiences, of course, the frustration and the nuisance situations occasioned by many children talking at once, by the incessant talker, or talking which interrupts and disturbs absorption. Nevertheless we are, in spite of assertions to the contrary, afraid of talking as an activity to which children have free access, and some teachers still make rules about it, indicating even if they do not mean to do so, that talk should on the whole be the prerogative of the teacher and of the child only when asked to speak out. Here, however, the exchange of talk is as essential as the medicine and care in illness; there must be conversation when other children may read and write.

What then are the problems for a child who in earliest years is not exposed to a rich environment of language? Such children have limited vocabulary because they have experienced little, and because their poverty of surrounding stimuli have made their expressive needs limited too. The assimilation of language begins very early in life and deprivation from the first moments of life in the outside world has long-term consequences. A child who has lacked experiences of everyday life and of the spoken word in abundance, is not ready to begin school, and certainly is not prepared to tackle the task of word recognition in written form. Deprived children have often had little colour, possessions, care in the fostering of their talking efforts, or stimulation, for them to use sounds or words. There is evidence that this kind of deprivation affects language development more than any other aspect of developing personality.* The results of pre-school language deprivation have a snowballing quality. Once a child can read his vocabulary increases rapidly, but the child from a poverty-stricken environment in this sense, whose speech level is retarded, remains with a limited vocabulary, backwardness in comprehension, and, of course, reading disability.

A teacher judges children by what they say in answer to her questions and by their actions and responses. As the deprived

* M. L. Kelmer Pringle, *Deprivation and Education.*

child most often does not measure up here to others because of his lack of experiences, she naturally, but sometimes mistakenly, considers him lacking in ability. It is no wonder that such a child, lacking often a warm relationship with the teacher whom he does not please, lacking motivation, does not readily learn to read and does not participate fully in discussion. Then may begin anxiety, perhaps withdrawal from a world so full of problems. It is often not possible to know how much emotional difficulties have contributed to the language disability, but certainly the lack of ability to keep up with a teacher's expectations in the mastery of language in school produces anxiety which further inhibits and may develop to influence detrimentally the whole growth of a child's personality.

This factor, then, of language, and of the communication needs which make language essential and desirable to one, is basic in the development of any plan for the special education of deprived children in the environmental sense. Our less able children are very often environmentally deprived, so that language and all activity which will, because it leads to communication, help the development of word language, must be our great concern. The difficulties are such, however, that it may well be that conventional methods of teaching reading and writing are not suitable and that for a time other channels of communication are more useful and important. It is certain that talking is very important indeed and that this must be fostered in connection with all activity so that it is meaningful and rich and can compensate in part for time already lost whilst communication has been limited.

There are among these children those who do not so greatly lack language facility, but whose language is that of a subsocial environment. Teachers so often forget that their own or their acquired middle class use of language is not that of most of the children they teach. They must recognize difficulties which may exist even in the everyday medium of spoken communication. The children speak in the language with which they are familiar. They use "telly", "pub", "never-never", and words which may be to a teacher incomprehensible, "rude", or even obscene. The children's speech must be that of the home primarily, and any early indication that this is not acceptable will accent fear which probably already exists, and will inhibit this most important and widest open channel of communication. We are concerned with speech as the vehicle of communication first and foremost. With local accent, slang, lack of grammar or beauty, it can still be the carrier of thought and expression, and at this stage other factors are unimportant. The teacher must make the effort necessary for her to communicate with the children, she must switch to their wavelength and come to understand their lives so that she may encourage and expand their existing level of vitality.

Some children come from homes where conversation does not take place often, as in the rural cottage or mining home where father may come in tired and silent and words do not flow freely. Many belong to homes where talk is not ordered conversation but is mainly the shouting of curses and instructions. There is not talking about things, and the thought-provoking, stimulating exchange which should be taking place in school and home. Many children tend to make sentences which are short and unfinished, conjunctions are repeated, nouns shortened, and nick-names used. Sometimes children tend to shout. They come from a background where people shout and they are frequently the objects of shouting. They may speak with extreme hesitation, without fluency, without resources of words, and without confidence. Often, of course, they have speech defects. In spite of all this they must receive only encouragement to speak, to listen to others and to speak again. The teacher is the mediator, the person who hèlps, always positively, accepting the speech offered, and not correcting until it is safe to do so without hurt or hindrance.

So often understanding of words remains distorted for a child because a teacher never really finds out that the child does not understand. Children endure patiently the morning assembly and lengthy "talks", much of which they cannot understand, without complaint, usually not giving any indication

unless a teacher probes, that there is any lack of understanding. One such teacher did ask her remedial children about
assembly when they returned one morning to the classroom.
"Could be Chinese, as far as I can tell", said one senior girl.
There followed a discussion about the meaning of the word
"pause", which had come before a hymn or notice. It is important
then to talk back, teacher to child, and child to teacher, and to
the class, to use many ways of stimulating speech, so that words
freely emerge in many contexts. For instance, words as stimuli for
dance, drama, painting, and modelling provide means of helping
children to be sure of meanings.

There may have been for some of these children absence from
school, difficulties of seeing or more particularly hearing, perhaps
unnoticed at a very early stage, or circumstances of teaching
which have meant for a child lack of understanding or stimulation
leading to verbal disinclination. Children learn in individual
ways and a single approach cannot be satisfactory for all children
in a large group. Classes are mostly too large for the ordinary
teacher to ascertain difficulties and deal individually with them
so as to prevent a child who is struggling from being left behind.
Focusing attention is necessary for the process of language
assimilation to take place. A tired, unwell, or poorly motivated
child does not pay attention. There is not comprehension. Where
writing is concerned there may even be difficulty in the actual
holding and manipulation of a pen or pencil, especially where a
child has poor motor co-ordination.

In considering language difficulties one has to take into account
the general ability of the child, his emotional freedom to learn,
his state of maturation, and the opportunities which he has to
practise with the amount of language he has already acquired.
There seems often to be a combination of difficulties. Any lack of
ability to use words, to know their meaning, and to grasp the
construction of language is a great barrier to learning. Whilst
most of the difficulties in acquiring and using spoken and written
language have for these children arisen from deprivation of
environment where language is concerned, and in general circum-

stances of normal living, there are still some for whom speech, reading, and writing are difficult and appear to be blocked, whose environment has not been impoverished, and others whose spoken communication is reasonably fluent but for whom reading and writing present great difficulty.

There is the condition of disturbed neurological organization which manifests itself in the inability to integrate the meaning of writing. This has been and is the subject of research at this present time.* The problems involved overlap those with which we are concerned in the school or class for educationally less able children and the results of research work at this level will be of great value to all children with varying degrees of language problem. In the school for the educationally subnormal and in our special classes, we have on the whole, children whose reading, writing, and speaking problems are related to over-all language poverty, and when considering ways of teaching these children a major concern must be the finding and using of channels of activity and understanding which will ease the way to language comprehension and use for these children.

As we have seen, one of the marked features, standing out clearly when one visits these schools and special classes and groups, is that of speech difficulty. There is lack of clarity and inability to pronounce some sounds, often amounting to unintelligible speech, and varying degrees of hesitation, erratic quality, and stammer. A very large number of less able children are poor speakers.

The ability to speak well varies considerably among the whole population. There are very fluent speakers, very bad stammerers, and all ranges between, in all sections of the community. The factors which contribute to a person's speech ability, to his clarity and fluency are many, environmental and neurological. Where the children we discuss are concerned, perhaps the high incidence of speech disorder is explained by the environmental poverty of good, fluent, clear speech, by the emotional instability which

* For example, research on dyslexia directed by Professor P. Meredith, University of Leeds.

is so prevalent among them, and by their lack of comprehension and security where word language is concerned. Often speech difficulty is rooted in anxiety, the child speaking more clearly and freely when with other children, when talking to a pet, a toy, or simply to themselves. There are many stammerers among these children as one would expect, but stammerers occur in all groups. Many of our least able children exhibit the sheer inability to shape words audibly and many lack the ability to continue fluently even for a phrase or sentence. Some defective speech patterns are well established by the time a child reaches school age.

Sometimes one finds among these children a child with some degree of physical malformation of the mouth, jaw, or teeth, which is directly related to the speech difficulty, but such cases are not frequent. Speech defect is sometimes related to hearing disability in these groups, but the speech problem is very great and widely spread.

Speech therapists do accomplish a great deal, especially when they establish good relationship with an individual child or small group. For these children the relief of speech defects often lies chiefly in the overcoming of the intense insecurity, lack of comprehension, and poverty of motivation for communication.

It is possible that the establishment of intense rhythmic sense, of the enjoyment of sound through choral speaking, singing, movement, and dance have a prominent part to play in this rehabilitation. The possible effect of expressive activities, bringing absorption, enjoyment, and freedom, upon this area of difficulty is important and will receive attention later. It is sufficient here to say that what is obviously necessary is that ways are found to help these children to talk and to overcome the fear and disinclination many develop to use their inadequate speech.

Given an atmosphere which is conducive to harmony of relationships and lack of fear, the less able child often proves to be much more voluble than one previously supposed. The group must not be too large. Ten children in a talking group are already too large a number. Everyone must, as they are ready, be able to have a share in conversation. Children with speech difficulty need encouragement and patience on the part of the whole group so that they may have courage to express themselves in spite of the knowledge that they keep the group waiting. Talking must be a central activity for these children; as they work with their hands, in intervals between activities, as well as times when a teacher deliberately provokes discussion. The teacher must be the sharer of talk, encouraging the timid, gently suppressing the over-voluble, and ready always to stimulate, praise, and clarify. There will always be things to talk about. This is the teacher's responsibility. Once a talking habit is formed conversation will arise, readily stimulated by activity, environment, feelings, and attitudes, however simple.

The shape of a group which talks together is important. Some shapes make for communication, as does the circle. A classroom must be a place arranged or, better, not arranged, so that members of the group are able to talk with others and with the teacher, unless for some reason they choose to retire to a quiet spot. Quiet is, of course, important. There must be moments when complete absorption brings about complete quiet, as in some dance or dramatic activity, when watching a film, listening to music, or to a story, and there must be a place where a child can be quiet if he so wishes.

This ready habit of interchange of talk may not at first arise, especially if it has been inhibited previously. It will take time, and much encouragement, particularly for conversation with social awareness to develop. Gaps in the talk will exist, some children will remain silent for some time, some will become aggressive talkers and will need gentle suppression, but there will be planning, talking to follow activity, words becoming more and more familiar tools which they handle with more and more confidence.

The tape recorder is a useful instrument for these children, to be used of course with the discrimination of a sensitive teacher who never willingly hurts or discourages. It can bring about acute attention, a dynamic interest, and has an immediacy which for these children is especially valuable. The spoken word on radio, gramophone record, film, and television is useful, and particularly important is the quality, clarity, and expressiveness of the teacher's own voice. Above all the children's speech and conversation must grow in confidence alongside their happiness and security, linking with occasions of enjoyment, and granting them self-confidence because they have the dignity of speaking to listeners.

CHAPTER 9

THE TEACHER

A Teacher has as his subject life and mind.
A Teacher's life is in living beings, not in printer's ink.
A Teacher is an Artificer of mind and noble life.
Above all, a Teacher never let a single life of those put into
      his hands be spoiled, or wasted, or flung
      aside through neglect, or scorn.
A Teacher is the helper and friend of the weak.
That is a Teacher.*

"I mean liking—indeed, loving—each individual child for himself
alone, and letting him know it.†

More important than anything else in the provision of education for children, and especially for the less successful child, is
the human being who may be not only teacher but in many cases
parent substitute, responsible for the growth of a child's personality so that he can take a place in his community on terms with
his fellows; or in part responsible for a social misfit, a delinquent
or weak creature, hurt and withdrawn, or aggressive and venge-
ful. It is a severe responsibility for any teacher, far greater than
that of getting a pupil through A-level examinations; yet still
there exists a pattern which provides the poorer teacher for the
poorer pupil. The poorer teacher with very important exceptions
goes to the poorer area, the less experienced teacher to the low
streams and even to the special remedial department. Colleges
of education often wisely send students from college with a very
low teaching grade indicating that this teacher needs help and

* Quoted in *Education*, 1954–64, West Riding Education Committee, from
Rev. Thring, *Theory and Practice of Teaching*, 1st edn., 1883, p. 117.
  † D. Wills, *Throw away thy Rod*, p. 138.

supervision, only to find that he or she has been given a C or D stream. At the present time accent lies in the field of administering the educational system; the dangers of measurement of children and teachers and the race for monetary reward loom very large. As a "remedial teacher" recently pointed out, there is little future prospect as far as promotion is concerned for the person who devotes himself to these special children. There are only a few headships of special schools and a few posts carrying major allowances.

How can we maintain, in this climate, teachers who really care and whose first question is not "How much allowance is this worth?" It is a shock to find in one school a sorting of teachers and classes by the drawing of lots, and in another an apology from the head for giving a teacher the "lowest" stream, coupled with the promise that it will not happen again for a while.

Fortunately there are teachers who really wish to teach these children and those teachers who go to special schools do on the whole belong to this category, as do many who make the class for the least academic children the happiest in some schools. There is still disparity, however, in our school system, in remuneration, and in esteem between those who teach the academically able and those who teach the least able of the children who come within the care of the education service. Our liveliest, most gifted teachers should be with the least able children if they have the desire and sympathy necessary, and at this present time, as an emergency measure, with our least able senior pupils.

Teachers of children who have such individual difficulties and who are likely to face so many problems must be secure and widely intelligent enough to teach creatively, with spontaneity, and immediacy, using opportunities as they arise and dealing with frustrations without undue tension. They must be experienced enough to be able steadily to use their own gifts and abilities to the full, to make use of that which they have and are. Such qualities cannot be with the youngest or with the least able of teachers, or with those who have themselves too great burdens or problems in their own professional or personal lives. We need lively, adventurous teachers who are disappointed but not afraid if a project fails, who take failure honestly and use it.

Much of the teaching of the less able child is harmed by half-adapted traditional methods, a hangover from a teacher's own schooldays. This is in part a condemnation of the college of education where so much remains theoretical and cannot become reality because it is not integrated into the practical task of teaching. It is even more a condemnation of the school situation met by a young teacher, insecure and searching, in her first post.

The least able children are so often regarded with contempt by "hard-boiled" members of staff. "These your children?" asked a supplementary course student in a department for teachers of educationally subnormal children. "Yes", answered the teacher proudly. "And the best of British luck to you," replied the mature student. Here were two attitudes. One person, dedicated and sincere, was shocked and hurt by the other, however light-hearted the intention, the attitude of a mature teacher engaged in the study of the nature of backwardness!

Sometimes when children in special classes are badly behaved, have become difficult to interest, and almost impossible to teach, they are naturally feared by some teachers. Most members of staff, faced with the formidable task of even a short time with such a class, resort to occupying them with safe tasks, proved by others to succeed in keeping peace; copying from a board, tidying cupboards; humdrum, repetitive tasks which produce a bored sullen kind of quiet. The teacher does not have courage enough to take a risk, even if she knows that there are ways in which the pupils could be brought to creative and worth-while activity and thought. The period of transition would be uncomfortable, even unpleasant, and would be likely to be accompanied by criticism and scorn from colleagues. These children have perhaps become problems. They did not begin that way. The barrier has arisen through continual frustration in the classroom and rejection in the life of the school. Teachers do so much want to "teach", and the less able children often reject this approach because it does not meet their understanding and even less their

A.S.M.—E

need. The children suffer tremendous frustration and punishment and scorn, and set up a greater barrier to learning.

Not much is expected of these children. A young teacher, given the task of teaching all subjects except science, woodwork, and games to a first-year class of "doubtful ability" in a comprehensive school, writes:

> The fact is, I kept them quiet enough, they were successfully contained, so I must be doing a good job. It might have been different if we had made more noise still.
>
> I did not feel, however, that anybody could feel proud of the year's work, educationally speaking, and I was puzzled by the praise we received from the authorities.*

Teachers of less able children, even more than teachers in ordinary classes, need to care enough for the relationship between them and the children to be warm and generous. A teacher must know the children as individual people, must project her feeling and understanding, and be personally involved with each one. She must have a combination of skill and love with which to deal with their problems and difficulties. She must not be afraid of affection, even if it produces from the younger child sometimes a caress or a kiss. There are, of course, limits to the amount of physical affection a teacher can permit when there are many children, but there is tremendous need for the brief demonstration of affection sometimes from a child, especially in a residential school. A teacher must also not be afraid when a child in such a group shows destructive urges. A good environment for these children gives opportunity for games, adventurous activities, drama, and dance, all of which help to give vent to aggressive and destructive tendencies in positive ways. Teachers are often afraid of extremes, of intense feeling, of high praise, of decisive judgement. In a school for educationally subnormal children one is faced often with extreme behaviour, and a teacher must expect it and meet it.

Sometimes a teacher who has herself experienced failure has a more ready understanding of the hurt and bitterness which might be within a child. Most teachers have been reasonably

* 'Neighbourhood school', A Schoolteacher, *New Society*, June 1966.

successful, especially in school, and it is hard for them to feel with a child who cannot succeed with letters and figures.

These children need more than others to belong, and for them especially the persistent presence of their teacher is very important. A vital factor for them is the stability of the people around them, the teachers, domestic staff, and housemothers. They need to "own" them, to depend upon their presence, and to know when they will be away.

Teachers must have knowledge of the history of the children they teach. So often the class teacher does not know the medical and family history of a child. Reasons for this kind of secrecy are obvious, but surely if the teacher is to be trusted with the care of a child she should also be trusted with the history of his difficulties.

It is certainly helpful if teachers in special departments and schools have a basic understanding of the psychology and sociology of education so that they may be intelligently aware of the problems with which they are involved. They should be teachers who understand the handicaps from which some children suffer, and who have studied, given thought, and have experienced, if possible, the sociological problem situations which lie behind the tragedies of some children. One is surprised so often at the ignorance of teachers about the physical condition of children in their classes. They cannot be medically trained, but one could ensure that they have knowledge of the manifestations of brain damage and of other physical disorders which occur, resulting in or existing alongside educational subnormality, and that school doctors make it part of their task to inform the teachers about a child's difficulty.

There must be among the teachers of these children some who have exceptional qualities, sometimes even eccentricities, which will break through the barriers of failure and culture to reach avenues which remain open. A teacher may be a reformer, furiously, aggressively on the side of the children, defending, perhaps at times over-supporting. Such a person may infuriate her colleagues but may well reach the needs of some children. Teachers who come themselves from underprivileged backgrounds could become excellent teachers of these children, because they would so immediately understand; unfortunately many such teachers tend to reject their kind. Teachers who are consistent, quiet, and steady, accepting all events with the same even-temperedness, are often successful. So many religious sisters have these qualities. They are devoted, yet not gushing or over impulsive, and the quiet sureness brings a secure atmosphere within which fear and aggressiveness disappear.

Children must be accepted and respected, not measured into failure and not living at the mercy of a cynical or despising tongue, or able to ride rough-shod over a weak or naïve teacher.

A teacher must develop insight into herself and into others. She will be sometimes inspired and will trust her inspiration. She will know the value of moderate anxiety and will tolerate it as valuable.

Every teacher does a better job with some children than with others. Always there will be successes and failures. It is the exceptional teachers who are necessary for the subnormal children—exceptional for their devotion, inspiration, and for their capacity to care and to understand.

Later we will discuss the kinds of avenues which might well be more used to help learning. The ways in which teachers teach, the kinds of activities they choose, and their own abilities and knowledge are very important; but it is the quality of the person that matters in this sphere of education beyond all specific ability.

Where can we find such teachers? We can recruit them from all our resources of trained teachers. Unfortunately, recruiting discriminately is difficult at a time of such acute shortage. For this same reason extra training for teaching in this special field must be limited. Teachers who have had special training must be better equipped in knowledge of the children and in the skills of teaching with regard to learning difficulties. I have found many of these mature students, however, too set already in their ideas both about children and about learning; and I wonder if such training could not come for many at a much earlier stage. Many young students in college are extremely interested and have the qualities which are necessary for this special teaching. Some do well on teaching practice in special schools and classes, and it would seem to be advisable that these young teachers, after some experience in the ordinary school, should be followed up so that they receive further training. There is usually a place for teachers of all kinds who have a desire to teach in this special situation. Variety of gift and of knowledge is always valuable, but help is needed for many teachers in these schools, so that they may have a child-centred approach which is so necessary, and the knowledge and facility to bring exploring, expressive, and creative activity to their teaching. Those who have been trained for primary school work have already a fund of knowledge and the fundamentals of a suitable approach. Many teachers who have had experience with very young children have, however, to realize that children who are in special departments and schools because they have learning problems are not infants and the infant school approach cannot simply be transferred.

It is necessary that both men and women enter this field. Women come more naturally, as in fact they do to the teaching profession, but especially where a school is residential it is important that there is a balance of men and women adults. In a boys' school there are matron, housemothers, wives, and domestic staff; a girls' school can be almost entirely a female world.

The problem of teachers living in residence arises. The teacher in a special department in a day school has her contact with her colleagues and her home life. A teacher in residence could have a very restricted existence, too close to such continual demands. Free time may not coincide with that of friends and she may centre her life too much around the children. The unmarried woman teacher in the residential school must take pains to see that her life is broad and that her contact with the outside world is rich. This is as important for the children as for herself.

One occasionally comes across a teacher who has herself difficulties of personality, or unhappy circumstances which have affected her own life. She attempts to find an outlet here for her own troubles or frustrations. This does sometimes work for both the children and herself, but it is a dangerous situation and needs careful observation on the part of a head. Giving of one's energy and care to help others can alleviate one's own distress in a most positive way; but I observed some cases where personal trouble had produced fearful, tense, and over-restricting teachers.

There arises a problem where specialist teachers are involved. In a special department in a secondary school it is good if the children concerned can share the special abilities and the facilities afforded in such subjects as physical education, music, and house-craft. In doing so they become more fully a part of the school. Unfortunately there are too many specialist teachers who cannot or do not wish to teach these children. One hears the physical education specialist, who could and often does contribute so much, say "They cannot be in teams, they are not reliable". The music specialist wants good music, the housecraft teacher finds them slow, and too often with the specialist teachers they become badly behaved through lack of interest and care.

In a special school there are all the visiting people who form part of the school community, the doctor, the nurse, and too rarely the physiotherapist and the speech therapist. In most special schools these people are welcome friends, bringing in a freshness from the outside world and breaking routine in a pleasant way. Theirs is an easier task; they see the children for a short time; they encounter mainly friendship and affection which these children give so readily.

Special schools for educationally subnormal children are, it seems, too rarely visited by education officers and specialist advisers. Sometimes a particular member of the advisory team has a special interest in the school, but too frequently a head will say that they do not often see "the people from the office" unless a county authority has an adviser for special schools who cares particularly for them.

The schools which I visited, without exception, welcomed visitors. The teachers seemed on the whole anxious to show their work and were undisturbed at having a stranger in the classroom. The heads always were welcoming and eager to show their school in detail. The children, always in my experience, found visitors an incentive to talk and to show things. They were hosts and hostesses of the highest quality. It was as if there was need on the part of staff and children to communicate with the outside, to be recognized and praised, and this after all is a human need.

The teaching of slow learners, backward or subnormal children, is an exacting and often a seemingly unrewarding task. There can be setbacks so frequent that a teacher may well become disheartened, and it is no wonder that the weaker ones sink into a hardened, routine existence which is destructive to teaching of any kind.

Teachers in schools and departments for these children need praise and encouragement as much as the children themselves undoubtedly do. The rewards are slow and not easily recognizable; and advisers, educationalists, and staffs of colleges of education could all play a part in the encouragement and help given to the teachers in this sphere. They need more time to recover from effort and more "nourishment" to equip them for a task which is so demanding.

PART II

CHAPTER 10

EXPLORATION, CREATION, AND COMMUNICATION

To see a world in a grain of sand
And heaven in a wild flower
Hold infinity in the palm of your hand
And eternity in an hour.*

Having to some extent stated the problem, it is necessary to consider what might be done to add to and change some of the present thought and action which is being devoted to the teaching of the less able children by so many people at this time. Nothing relevant which can be said is completely new. In some classrooms there are individuals who succeed with educationally subnormal children especially well in some area or areas of learning, by a particular approach. It is important that everything that is likely to be profitable for these children is made known and used, that more teachers might make life fuller for them, and ensure that they contribute to the utmost to the society in which they will live.

An educationalist of great experience in this field said that his main desire for these children was that they should become independent adults and that they should keep out of the hands of the police. These children are personalities with individual potential for happiness and delight, for liking and loving, and for giving, especially to the next generation so that they in their turn may not be in such need.

We must know as much as possible about the factors that cause failure for some children. There is no severe boundary between

* W. Blake, Auguries of Innocence, *Poets of the English Language*, vol. 4, p. 18.

the so-called slower learner or remedial child and other children. We know the importance of the environment of the very young child and the power of early and initial learning. "The nature of the individual's pursuit of life, liberty and happiness may be largely determined by the nature of the environmental conditions under which he has lived in his formative years."*

Environment has a great effect upon attainment. It is beyond the capacity of a teacher to directly alter the home environment of a child, but we could try to make the school environment as compensatory as possible, in simple loveliness, liveliness, order, and care. School buildings in deprived areas are often sadly as drab and uninspiring as the housing, but this may be remedied as a priority measure. Deprivation arising from the lack of security, love, and care which come from good parents and family relationships may find some alleviation in some places if we can establish welfare services to watch over the troubles in some families where children suffer. Publicity has been given of late to poverty and malnutrition existing in this affluent community, and it may be that this will receive attention. Some aspects of environmental deprivation, however, can be eliminated only by educating future generations of parents so that they will not make for their children deprived homes. Indeed, there is evidence that a good school environment and a teacher, influencing a child vitally, can through the child, influence the home from which he comes.

Where there is brain damage a teacher must understand as fully as possible, and strive to find and to help the child to use all available avenues of development, so that these may fulfil their own purpose and compensate if possible for others.

Can we make education therapeutically powerful enough to overcome the increasing limits to change as a child becomes older? Can we do more to make sure that adequate attention comes to the child in need of it while he is very young? Can we re-channel his characteristics and abilities, teach him to use them, and take away his fear? "The purpose of education is not to produce

* B. Bloom, *Stability and Change in Human Characteristics*, p. 13.

more scholars, technicians, and job hunters, but integrated men and women who are free of fear, for only between such human beings can there be enduring peace."*

One must, of course, consider the immediate practical issue upon which my colleague concentrated when he spoke so rightly of independence and keeping these children out of the hands of the police. They have to enter a tough, adult world and must be prepared for the factory floor, shop, market garden, or farm, and for the life around them. They have to learn to withstand, when necessary, advertising persuaders and plausible friends, to judge for themselves, to cope with the formalities of living in a welfare state, to handle money, to travel about in a world of speed and danger, to live with time to spend in ways of their own choosing, and to shoulder the responsibilities of adult life in all its aspects.

All these issues, however, will be handled adequately only if a child grows as a personality, fortified as fully as possible for living, for work, and for leisure. "The greater the number of people who prove to be educable beyond all previous expectation, the stronger the suspicion grows that the rest may have been underestimated also."†

We must, whilst looking realistically at their difficulties, have faith in these children and search carefully for avenues whereby they can develop further towards communication, understanding, and maturity, in this society. If possible we must help them to become literate. In this culture this becomes increasingly important, although the reasons for this are not at all clear. Nevertheless, we must not treat literacy as a trick to be implanted; literacy must develop with experience and understanding, and with the need and desire to communicate, and other ways must be available whilst reading and writing are not.

Let us speak now of relationships. There is with these children the battle to "become", which exists at least for a time. It is true that such a desire may become submerged or dormant,

* Krisnamurti, *Education and the Significance of Life*, p. 15.
† *Half our Future*, the Newsom Committee Report, H.M.S.O., 1962, p. 14.

defeat being too often or too heavily suppressing, but there is with most of the children who fail in school markedly, the pain of not "becoming", the ache of wanting to be something which they do not feel that they are. Experienced teachers who have had among more successful children in each year, a few who failed, when asked about channels to learning for these children said:

> They want affection and notice, they thrive on appreciation and attention and in the atmosphere of a small group they manage to make progress. I think the succession of callers at my room inquiring for jobs and the time I spend with them watering the plants is an important cog in the school wheel. It is amazing how they will help each other. One must give them things to do for you, to help, to be of use.

This relationship to people is the nourishment of the emotions, necessary for the personality to grow and for the energy to spark, necessary for children's learning. One sees the result of lack of warmth of feeling in children who have been brought up in institutions with an institutional atmosphere or who have had lack of a modicum of parental love and care. How much have we fostered courtesy which demands non-communication? "How are you?" "Very well thank you." We must show discretion, tact, and modesty, not talk too much, or display feeling too freely.

Children are imaginatively free and undominated by human pressures as perhaps they never are again. Never again are relationships so vital. Some children who fail in class fail also as members of the school community. They suffer, to a lesser extent perhaps, as does the deaf child, the autistic child, the partially sighted or blind, or those in isolation for any reason. They are deprived of that vital spark which is the essence of the contact between their inner selves and the outside world. They are only half alive, and this quite naturally affects the personal and social growth, the development of play, imagination, awareness of the relatedness of things, and, of course, communicating language. The evidence is in the faces and bodies of such children. There is lack of vitality. We may try to teach these children mechanically to communicate as we seem to teach the deaf child, but it is life with people, and a place with people that is important. We must bring these children to life, with care, with love, using all means available to make them play their part, and to make them emerge.

Communion comes about and understanding grows when we meet on the same level at the same time. We must make it possible particularly for these children to have relationships with confidence. Attitudes of inwardness will breed for them more inwardness. They must communicate to know themselves. There is the need to give, "to have a hand in", to be a part of life which is going on around. We know the necessity for people to be with people, to talk, to argue, to contribute, to be accepted as a contributor, to be worth something. One sees a personality emerge in company, one knows how some people need to talk and talk, even on the telephone, one meets the moment of a child's outburst after a long silence.

Teachers tend to be shy of relationships, and for these children often the teacher is a very necessary relation. They must become people who belong and are respected as individuals, who know and feel that this is so, and who give respect and recognition to others. With recognition and mutual respect comes dignity, which they may well have had little chance to perceive or acquire, and positive attitudes are developed with self-awareness.

They need to make effort and to recognize it, to have joy in doing, and to become aware of success and earned praise. There is great need for the teacher to be on the same side, to make things safer when new steps are taken, to be seen to believe in the adventure, and so to set the child free to proceed. "The earth has its own pulse and rhythms and the wise and fortunate man leans into the wind, sows with the season, and searches for water in valleys where water flows."*

"Maturity", said John Murray, "is of first consequence in education."† He describes maturity as the beginning of having one's centre outside oneself, when emotions are capable of being

* H. Burland, *High, Wide and Lonesome.*
† Television appearance, B.B.C., 11 November 1965.

objective, when one becomes a person in relationship to others. This growing maturity must involve aggression and rebellion sometimes, and will not be persistent harmony arising out of sensitivity and sympathy in a steadily proceeding relationship. One must expect anger and frustration as with everybody, one must expect separation from, as well as unity with, teacher and fellows. But growth in relationship is vitally important for these children who in their struggle with life and with education, remain so often very immature socially. They will grow up through relationships if we can give them the confidence to make them, and the belief in themselves and others.

> Wherever things and people make demands of us, wherever we require something from things and people, whatever we find a genuine interest in, there value lies.*

> Communication begins with a natural interchange of specific energies enabling creatures to control one another's behaviour.†

There is involved in communication the whole repertoire of the senses, some understanding and organizing of experiences, excitement about them, and radiative behaviour. There is necessity for sender and receiver, suitably tuned to each other.

Whatever the mechanics of communication, there must be involvement with life. Communication in primitive societies is concerned with all available activity: eating, sex, fighting, magic, dancing, acting, painting, modelling, sound, and rhythm. Human beings shape and form the means of expression, creation is involved, and man becomes artist.

Society depends upon communication and a person cannot be a member of society without it. The process must be complete; one cannot ignore that which is around one and retain the outgoing, contributing factor which gives membership. "Blind eyes do not see, neither do they reveal."‡

The most important factor then, concerning the enrichment of communication for these children especially, is the factor of

* M. Hourd, *The Education of the Poetic Spirit*, p. 159.
† P. Meredith, *Instruments of Communication*, p. 56.
‡ M. Hourd, *op. cit.*, p. 39.

living, of being alive in a living environment, of sensation through a lively body and an active personality, of dynamic cognition and expression.

In all education there is the important factor of vitality. Where there is energy, curiosity, interest and excitement, will and persistence, and the capacity for feeling, enjoyment, and love, learning is likely to be taking place. There are most certainly factors of personality traits, incentive, faith, and training, overlapping and impossible to estimate fully, which are responsible for vitality in a person's behaviour. When, however, we consider the major importance of every single aspect which might contribute to, or distract from, success for a child whose adequacy in his society is in doubt, we must regard each factor.

First let us consider the physical aspects of vitality. We know that the healthy, lively body is more likely to house an active mind than the sick and ailing one. We do not know how much compensation for a sick body a single person may produce from rich resources of personality. A healthy child, free from disease, adequately nourished, rested, active, and stimulated by fresh air, is likely to have lively senses, and, one would think, would go in search of experiences. It is evident that many of the children who are not succeeding in our educational system are suffering from a subnormal level of physical health. We have seen in past chapters the evidence of physical deformity, sensory loss, undersize and obesity, poor circulation, and respiratory trouble which many of these children exhibit. Many of them are poorly nourished and have poor living conditions. Sedation has been mentioned as necessary but crippling treatment for some of these children. Children are devitalized by over-feeding, over-clothing, lack of physical exercise, and fresh air, and addiction to television and cinema.

There is then for the children being studied a major chance that there will be factors of physical subnormality which contribute to lack of vitality, learning drive, and the whole process of communication. These physical factors would seem to be the most obvious and the easiest to remedy, and certainly in special schools this is being done to a great extent. Just as these children need nourishing in every aspect of their education, there must be particular "physical nourishment", not only good food and cleanliness, rest, and medical care, but graduated opportunities for acquiring bodily strength, and the stimulation of fresh air and exercise. These children will often not have the initiative to go to the swimming bath in the town or to set out on a walking expedition, to tackle something which demands a little more than they think they can give. They will have to be led more to the opportunities which provide for the joys of freedom, activity, and endurance in physical things.

When one attempts to grasp the failing qualities characterizing the less able children, one is aware of an aura of weakness which, arising as it does from a combination and co-ordination of cause and effect, forms a barrier between the life which surrounds them and themselves.

If one tried to divide people into the stronger and the weaker, which fortunately would be an impossible task to perform with worthwhile accuracy, most of these children would fall into the "weaker" category. We all have a share of strength and weakness, but the stronger tend to become stronger and the weak weaker. We have among special children many who react to situations with weakness. Often they are sensitive of their own inadequacy, apt to become flustered and unsure, to lose confidence quickly, and to perpetuate their own failure.

How easy it is to add to this weakness by making such children feel small! How greedy and insensitive the strong often are, and the strong often include the teacher! Somehow some teachers do not expect the "bottom class" to be even aware that they are being treated as unimportant members of the community. They can be turned out of the hall, deprived of their drama, dance, or physical education, because of an examination or play rehearsal in which they take no part, they can be "taken" by a senior girl or prefect to be amused in some sedentary way, but are seldom thanked for tolerating their neglect. It is little wonder that so often they are not tolerant.

It is not easy to define sadness, dejection, defeat, or despair, and it is impossible to know how they are registered and have effect for any individual child, but most certainly they do not bring self-respect and animation which foster communication. Every defeat and fear nourishes others and so we get reactions which are predominantly weak; inhibition, inertia, weariness, escapism, withdrawal, self-pity, and silence—in fact, lack of communication. Paul Tournier in his book *The Strong and the Weak* called it "turning the lights of life low".

Stronger reactions from the children are the outbursts of temper, even the perpetual cry of "unfair". At least these are active. These children need to have their fighting attitudes stimulated. With these they will begin to communicate. They need energy and attention, stimulated by interest, metabolism which is alerted, spontaneity brought to life and fostered, and vaso-motor reactions which are ready. Action creates the actor, the will set in motion.

They have to struggle and sometimes much time spent apathetically has gone by. Then the struggle is a mighty one. They need power to compensate dejection and to overcome the inferior aura in which they find themselves. The modern world is increasingly hard on the weak. The will to win triumphs over deficiencies in physique for the athlete often, the will to live can triumph over sickness. Certainly there is little triumph without it. Where are we to find this "will" for these children who need it so badly and in such good measure? Often their plight has been initiated by that very lack in their own mother or father.

There must be created the liveliness of the receptive state, unscreened by prejudice or fear. "Awareness is observation without condemnation", says Krisnamurti.* Consciousness itself is action and being aware is the beginning of understanding. This consciousness of being in a state of receiving is a vital state, not tied to necessity, but overflowing beyond the bounds of usefulness as play does, as the activity of children does. There must be surplus energy available, as in the child there is more physical

* Krisnamurti, *Life Ahead*, p. 173.

activity released than he actually needs for his development. There must be the capacity for play, the privilege to waste energy. Education needs always the play-like approach which sets free a surplus of vitality. From such expenditure is extracted a part which remains with the personality. We are in teaching too engrossed with that which is immediately useful or seems to be the next step. Just as surpluses have to exist in nature, in the production of seeds, and the variances of the weather, there must be such surpluses in the activity of a child, so that growth may take place.

So these children must learn to play. It must be for them a positive life, and one in which they can participate with that ability which they have, and with the contribution they can make. Life must be intelligible to them, school linking with their existence, not as subjects or skills or behaviour patterns which belong to school hours only. They need to be involved with ideas which are of their world; we must at all costs fill them with life.

> There is first and foremost the effective life, the life of the emotions. It is roughly in this sphere that the modern world most lets down its young people, for of course it is closely connected with the moral life as well; or to put it another way, it is highly relevant to the quality of our lives, with the realisation that in the intimacies of our day to day living it is possible to function at a variety of levels in accordance with the way in which our feelings are directed.*

Some think of imagination as a commodity granted to a few and denied to most, especially perhaps denied to the child who is a failure in school; some think of imagination as that useless part of a person which detracts from real learning, taking the mind off more worth-while things; a few see imagination as the "Universal and indispensable instrument of all levels of living in the human world".†

To allow the mind to be free and to stimulate the imagination is to give way to experiencing. For children there is wonder, surprise, mystery, and excitement. Deep and strong feelings are important and are needing to be evoked and expressed, not sup-

* G. H. Bantock, *Education in an Industrial Society*, pp. 210–11.
† H. Rugg, *Imagination*, p. 37.

pressed. The world of money, supermarkets, bingo, and constant television, is a world of non-feeling and superficial titillation.

If children experience with feeling they develop care and love. These are real and, far from taking a child to a false dreamland, bring him to reality. Imagination is personal—it belongs deeply to an individual. To use imagination is fundamental to a child as he grows to love, and to possess ideas, to deal with reality, and to understand. So we must feed the imagination with all the wealth at our disposal in the realm of education. Starving imagination is wasting human potential at all levels. Here in the area of this study it is probably the answer to learning stagnation, to the needs of self-respect, and self-discrimination, the sense of the goodness of life, and the contribution to be made to it.

Much is happening which is progressive in education; there are areas of activity and individuals which have startled the educational world. There are too many, however, who pay lip service to progressiveness, to freedom for the individual, to creativity, and the abandonment of recognized but rigid concepts; but who in practice do not allow these to happen, or who do not truly see what happens in their schools. Here again even our sincere striving for children's growth becomes entangled with the more tangible striving for power.

We tend to look hard at intelligence. In fact we must look far. Creativeness is a personal not an intellectual thing. Conventional education uses the stimuli of competition and success, anger, resentment and fear. Progressive education withdraws the "culling edge" of such incentives. Can we learn to use education for unknown ends? For the intellectually able the educational ends are only too clear; for the non-intellectual and the markedly less able child, the ends become much more difficult to ascertain. The teacher who, seeing a less able child's painting said "We shall have to do something about that", had certainly ascertained little.

> We see that to open anew a well of springing water, not to cleanse the stagnant tank, or fill, bucket by bucket, the leaden cistern; that the education of the intellect, by awakening the principle and method of self

development was his proposed object, not any specific information that can be conveyed into it from without, not to assist in sorting the passive mind with the various sorts of knowledge most in request, as if the human soul were a mere repository or banqueting room, but to place it in such relations of circumstance as should gradually excite the germinal power that craves no knowledge but what it can take up into itself, what it can appropriate, and reproduce in fruits of its own.

To shape, to dye, to paint over, and to mechanise the mind, he resigned as their proper trade, to the sophists, against whom he waged open and unremitting war.*

Coleridge speaks of slavery to the order.

What makes a slave a slave? If I mistake not it is oppression—it is the being in a state out of which he cannot hope to rise, and he who is placed where there is no motive for action but where the miserable thing he must ever remain in the same sphere, is a state and a pitiable one.†

Are many of these children in a state of slavery to their condition? We allow them to see nothing but difficulties in their way. Imagination offers such alleviation from this state; it removes and works around obstacles.

The mind and personality are to be "called forth", educated; awareness and consciousness enlarged, feelings and sensations fed and awakened, and fed again. There must be time to be in tune with that which is about one; time to be quiet, to feel and listen; to recognize and trust; for threads of relationships to be set in motion. Man is the slave of time. We have time and motion studies, the stop watch, the bell. In America companies have paid the passengers for every minute the express runs late. Man masters time. These children, like artists and mystics, must if possible be somewhat free from the throttling of time. Yet time in another sense for them is urgent; that we recognize their special need of our time, and that we recognize the urgency of using their earliest years.

There is the importance of pleasure which is linked so clearly with imaginative activity and with creation, however seemingly humble. Simple happiness is a situation of freedom; excitement and enthusiasm arise in discovery, much joy, and sheer love.

* H. D. Rankin, *Plato and the Individual*, p. 79.
† K. Coburn, philosophic lecture by Coleridge quoted in *Inquiring Spirit*, p. 35.

Emotions and states such as these create the conditions right for learning. We must stir the emotions which in our civilization are left so much to sleep or to be suppressed.

There is the world of the unconscious about which a teacher must speak with trepidation if he is to remain in the category of the "practical". Primitive man had need for the inner world. The African Bushman of human life as a whole said, "There is a dreamer dreaming us".* We have need of dreams, too, and of that inner, intangible self which needs ritual, which stores sensation, and deals in symbols. Poincaré slept hoping that his problem would evolve during his sleep; many know the solution of "sleeping on it". A child has need to become as involved as in his dreams, with the quality of things, with beauty and ugliness, with joy and some misery, with men and women, with opposites and similarities. It is difficult to explain a feeling or a dream or an intense enjoyment. This is where we need art involving many media, art which, "Now discouraged as a bungler, now glorified as a genius, and finally takes its refuge with those who leave it to its own devices".†

As children discover, relating feeling and thinking, recognizing, remembering, and forgetting, the "match maker", as Koestler expresses it, is the unconscious. They need the language of the symbol to feed this, and this the arts supply, uniting the external and the internal, supplying the link between thoughts and things.

The symbol, says Karl Jasper, "Catches what would otherwise stream out of us and be lost in the void. The symbol shows what, without it, would remain completely hidden from us. . . . Only he who recognizes the symbol becomes man."‡

There is a bleakness in the nature of so much of our school work for the less able child. They tend not to reach much that is joyful, exciting, where the imagination is really lit up. Children are individuals needing the right to choose, the right to be with creation, wonder, surprises, and to find kinship with things as

---

* A. McGlashan, *The Savage and the Beautiful*, p. 129.
† W. Grözinger, *Scribbling, Drawing, Painting*, p. 18.
‡ Karl Jasper, *The Nature of Psychotherapy*, p. 95.

their prerogative. They need these things, being human. As Philip Toynbee points out, only rare beings become saints by way of asceticism or benefit by deprivation.*

Imagination is destroyed so often by measurement and by fragmentation of experience. There is need for enormous provision for sensory experience, for activity and energy so that each child may feel the dignity of his being, and the process of grasping and possessing the richness of life, and of its knowledge. "That is why the ancients said the act of knowing is a properly immanent act, a perfectly vital action, belonging to the category 'quality'. . . . It is at once a condition and a means and an expression of that act."*

We are forced mercifully into a situation of setting about education for living itself; not for a particular function. It may well be that in this area, with the children who do not readily succeed, lie the agencies for change in our education and in our social life. Can we effect a real change at this level, giving self-awareness and self-knowledge to these children, pride and dignity to them as people, overflowing maybe to the homes from which they come, or at least to the homes which they will make. Only education can ensure the uplifting of people as social beings. We should really be grateful to those who find the processes of learning which we put before them difficult, because they may at least make us aware of the limitations of our attitudes and the need for universal culture.

We have spoken already of the qualities we need in our "special" teachers. At risk of repetition, the teacher of the less successful in our schools must become a person who can clear away the established patterns and anticipations of teaching so that he can really come to know the children, to take risks, to allow things to happen, and to take time, with trust and belief, in the quality of life itself. The reader must not become too worried because one speaks in such terms. Some ways which are extremely tangible will be brought forward. Exploration and creativity must have

* P. Toynbee in the *New Statesman*, October 1966.
† J. Maritain, *The Degrees of Knowledge*, p. 113.

signposts and some of these will be indicated. There must be, however, some teachers who are prepared to leave school mastering, tutoring, lecturing, "varnishing", and turn to educating.

Teachers have been accused of hanging on to ways and ideas, of not being ready to accept change, of not being willing or able to tackle that which is other than that which they know. In the case of the least able children in our schools, however, they are forced to look again and to accept that other ways than those established may be better. They should be ready to question the wisdom of even sense of some educational patterns and look to the future, hopefully and energetically, but with the thought of helping people of quality to grow from the lowest apparent ability in our schools.

> He must be apt to provoke, prompt to encourage, quick to pursue the startling and the unrehearsed. He must have the insight to discern and the patience to accept the power of the impromptu to transform the pattern of experience. With this awareness and this character the teacher will not be among those who collaborate with the quotidian in strangling the creature, or those who conspire with what is smothering what is to be. He will belong with those who, as Yeats said, are continually making and unmaking mankind.*

The second section of this book will be devoted to discussion and clarification of those activities which can play a large part in the education of the senses, imagination, and expressive faculties, so that channels of understanding might be opened up for the child who finds more used and perhaps more readily accepted ways of schooling less profitable than most children.

There will be discussion of the visual arts, movement, dance and dance drama, music, poetry, and story; all these particularly, and all areas of activity which involve the imagination most vividly. In order to clarify, discussion will take place where possible in defined areas, but in the school situation especially, there must be overlapping, choice of media, spontaneous changes from one medium of expression to another, and all the time the

* W. Walsh, *The Use of Imagination*, p. 242.

knowledge that the abilities of teacher and children and the circumstances of environment will influence the choice of expressive channel within which activity and interest begin to take place. Vitality of thought is dependent upon feeling. Appreciation, contemplation, and creative experience are closely linked and can be continuous. Success means the establishment of sentiments and attitudes, and with sympathy and encouragement, practical application, and personality growth. There must be used the wonder of the young child and the energy of the adolescent, and every chance when a positive attitude might be founded, so that when thwarted in one area another becomes available for a child. There will arise a general awareness of harmony, order and pattern around, of the rhythm and laws which lie beneath all arts and all life. The imagination made alive is concerned not yet with solving problems but with discovery. "The flash will not occur unless the mind, conscious and unconscious have been stored with a rich body of percepts, images, motor adjustments and concepts."*

These flashes can be possible for the child who is less successful than most in school, if we prepare the way especially carefully and richly. There will be aroused enthusiasm and energy, emotion, and further energy, even if such energy has sometimes to be used to surmount difficulties. There is the urge to run, leap, paint, cut, carve; communication need not be through words but through movement, paint, or sound. For some time, even a long time, it may be that a child expresses mainly through these media. Always there is a language. There need not be blockage in communication. Experience can come to order and understanding through the channels which are open.

A child will come to name things; to use more and more words. "What is it called? What is the word?" As with higher levels of creation there will be leaps in the dark when understanding, including the understanding of words takes place, and the links are established. No person sees exactly the same or understands in exactly the same way as another. Word language must become

* H. Rugg, *Imagination*, p. 13.

exciting for these children. The magic and excitement of words and names, as with earliest man, is irrepressible. A concept is incomplete without words which are partners.

Multi-dimensions of experience are necessary. Children create with whatever resources they have.

The arts are sources of education, stimulating the mind and body. They are not for pleasure only, but have reason in the pursuit of understanding. I propose that we set forth on an extensive programme of expressive activity for these children. "They have no imagination", many say. We must then feed the imagination through environment and experiences with the guidance of a generous finder of experiences.

We may or may not achieve literacy, but certainly we shall achieve for them more than by any other means available the happiness, experience of living, personal and social growth.

CHAPTER 11

THE RICH ENVIRONMENT

> For, on a table drawn beside his head,
> He had put, within his reach,
> A box of counters, and a red-vein'd stone.
> A piece of glass abraded by the beach.
> And six or seven shells,
> A bottle of bluebells
> And two French copper coins ranged there with careful art
> To comfort his sad heart.*

It is possible that only those children who are privileged in their homes and early environment, or those with exceptional compensatory qualities and circumstances can deal adequately with education as we offer it. One might wonder what the results might be if we enriched the educational programme for all with more food for the senses, expressive and aesthetic experience, having less accent upon the actual teaching of the skills of reading, writing, and number, and other accepted subjects of the school curriculum. Where there are children who are seen to be finding extreme difficulty in learning in school, however, there should be no objection to a radical rethinking of the means by which we offer them education. There would seem to be the possibility of gain and very little to lose.

As we have seen, a large proportion of these children have a home environment which is greatly deprived, if one considers only the conditions of comfort, cleanliness, order, beauty, and interest which surround them in their homes and everyday surroundings. One must say again that for a child to grow and develop harmoniously, physical surroundings are not, it seems,

* Coventry Patmore, The toys, *The Cassell Book of English Poetry*, no. 876.

the important factor. Witness the surprise one receives when perhaps one takes a child home ill and discovers the utter poverty of the surroundings which constitute a home for a clean, happy, apparently happy, and interested child. Love, acceptance, security, and opportunities for interaction with children and adults are much more important. Yet, if we are to help a child with learning difficulties, we must find ways to compensate for the impoverishment of the environment which should contribute to the stimulus, impetus, and material of learning. School environment must nourish abundantly. Some provision is made for the partially sighted, the deaf, the physically handicapped, even for those who learn with difficulty, but about those whose social upbringing is beset with handicap, we hardly know.

There is great need for co-ordination of departments dealing with social problems and especially for closer relationship and mutual trust between social workers and schools. Information comes to light in the press, on radio or television, such as that dealing with the disgraceful conditions under which children stay when "looked after" by unregistered child minders, the fostering of children, and conditions of slum homes, and is received with due shock by the almost disbelieving public. There is urgent need for a well integrated and organized family service, and this we hope will be the result of much recent publicity. How at this time however, can we enrich emphatically the environment for the child whose learning ability is suffering? "Man's desires are limited by his perceptions, none can desire what he has not perceived."*

A child in the remedial stream of a large secondary school, a neat, well-cared-for child, chatting about the cold weather, said that they had their coal delivered behind the armchair in the sitting room because if it were outside people would take it. "My dad," she said, "hasn't much room in that corner, but it can't be helped."

Often the house, although of recent structure, is in bad repair; there is little paint on the doors, wallpaper is torn and dirty,

* W. Blake, There is no natural religion, *Complete Poetry and Prose*, p. 147.

and there is an atmosphere of muddle and dullness even if there is moderate cleanliness. The house itself may be so derelict that the squalor and dirt may be almost inevitable. There may be tidiness with emptiness, order but no beauty, comfort, colour, or interest. A child may become to some extent impervious to the immediate effects of such surroundings. There is evidence that many do not, however. Senior girls wrote longingly, "I would like to have a win on the pools [spelt poste] and Buy a new House". "I would buy a three pees suite with cushins."

It is important then that the school surroundings compensate as vigorously as is possible for the home in which a child spends so much time. This is one of the more tangible ways through which we can help the situation of learning poverty.

Let us look first at the actual classroom and working spaces in which a child spends a large part of the school day, however progressive and lively the school programme may be. When one goes into an infant school, almost without exception, colour is abundant; there are plants, books, charts, models, paintings, perhaps an aquarium, and sometimes an indoor aviary. The whole place is rich with the products of the children's activities and with things of interest. Sometimes infant classrooms are so filled with materials that they are cluttered and confused. Nevertheless they are rarely stark, ugly, or dull. The junior school has often this atmosphere too, but many senior schools have bare classrooms without stimulus or interest.

Light, warmth, and colour are important and interrelated. Furniture should be light and portable and as good in design as is possible for the money available. The classroom must be as lovely a place as an essentially working area can be, where in parts mess can be made, but where a working order does prevail. There should be flowers and plants, places where there are displays and arrangements, orderly corners where books can be easily located. The children must have private cupboard and desk space, even wall space which belongs especially to each one of them. These are often children who have little of their very own, particularly space. Most important of all, the classroom should be a place which the children themselves make, with their paintings on the wall, taking at least pride of place, with their charts and wall folders, and their flower arrangements and designs.

The classroom will very likely be spoiled by children, until they learn to love and care for things. There is here a problem which heads and colleagues do not understand. "Please do not put new desks into my room," said a remedial stream teacher, "I know that they will get spoiled at some time and then what a row there will be." We shall have to bear with spoiling when it means that these children can have the pleasure of new unscathed things. Too often they have the already dirty and smudged furniture lest they should spoil something better. They most of all need the pleasure and incentive to care which lovely things can bring.

Barrenness often applies to the corridors, halls, and passage-ways of our schools. Some architects, within the limits allowed them by legislation and finance, go to great lengths, with pride, to see that school interiors are colourful and attractive, even if the outside of the school is difficult to redeem. There are schools housed in old, drab buildings in industrial areas, but the interior is lively with colour, best use being made of odd corners and the oddities of Victorian building. Some of these school interiors compensate as well as possible for the ugly homes of many children. One has, of course, to consider the relative needs of a school and money must be spent with care, but to give all children and teachers, especially those children from non-stimulating, empty homes, welcoming, pleasant surroundings would seem to be little to ask. This does not mean expensive statues and pictures or velvet curtains, but a home for education augmenting the personalities there and the relationships which are of major importance.

Space is important, especially for these children. Many live in cramped and overcrowded surroundings, which mean for the younger children little freedom of movement, and for the older children lack of privacy, a place to play major games or even to enjoy the sensation of some emptiness around one. In special schools where an old house or mansion has been transformed into a school, there is the serious lack of a large indoor space. Children must have the opportunity to move energetically and freely indoors, both from the point of view of release when weather makes it necessary to stay in and because movement education is for them very important. These children feel lost in a space which is very large as are some of our most modern gymnasia and the sports halls which at present exist in schools in America. They need a space which continues in spite of area to be welcoming and secure; such a hall space as we have in many of our newer schools.

Outdoor space is also very important. These children, more than most, need playgrounds which have seats, swings and climbing apparatus; they need also grass and trees and, if possible, adventure material, old cars, boats, tents, and building facilities. They need also gardens, things which are predominantly providing serenity and beauty, but which also provide things which grow.

The order, harmony, and flexibility of such working areas should extend to the dining room, the cloakrooms, and washrooms. The need is of course great for all children. One would wish that for the privileged child the school should be a place to which she delighted to come, but for the children we discuss the need is therapeutic. Eating for these children should be particularly a civilized, pleasant, social occasion, with plates, dishes, and cutlery of good design and colour, food tastefully served, in conditions of courtesy and friendliness. Every opportunity for communication, offering experiences of value is important. Mealtimes are very major in the lives of such children, and this time is likely to make a deep impression. Everyday habitual activities, such as washing and changing clothing, can be used to give experience of the pleasure of handling good utensils, in clean, pleasant surroundings, with relationships which build good standards, security, and confidence. In the residential school many opportunities are available for awakening and feeding sense awareness and regard for materials of everyday life.

The environment of school should be a home-like workshop, for talking about things, for searching, and discovering, for making things, sounds, music, plays, and dances.

Many schools, especially primary schools, have already such an environment, or at least some part of it. There is sometimes overestimation of the value of that which costs money in buildings and amenities. These essentials which the deprived child needs are often not extremely costly. One is asking much more for thought, care, and understanding than for money, and this especially for the children whose learning difficulties may be opened up and eased somewhat by the provision of better surroundings than are provided for many of this present time.

All schools are part of a village, town, or district. Everyone passes every-day familiar things; the environment is one of people as well as things. There are relatives, friends, neighbours, who become part of everyday life. Each day and night nature changes the atmosphere and the light so that always there is variation. Yet many people, even children, find little interest, no wonder or excitement in their surroundings.

Progressive teachers of English find it necessary to burn paper or blow bubbles to give children experiences about which they can write. Yet when looking through *The Excitement of Writing*, which quotes the expressive writing of children of various ages from a variety of schools and areas in the West Riding of Yorkshire, I found the following titles; *The Playground, At the Hairdresser, My Dog, Windfall Apples, Morning in the Allotments, Our Street at Night, At the Baths, The View from the top of Car Lane, The Tree, In the Firelight, The Fire, Market Day, Our Back Street*. Also, *My Day, My Mother, An Interesting Character*, and *Snow, Floods, Rain, Catkins, Tulips, Frost, Winter Colours, A Hot Day*, and *A Misty Morning*.

These children had been awakened to look at their surroundings. They had not found them dull.

OUR BACK STREET

From the old blackening shop hung a torn, dirty advertisement, limp and wet after a shower of rain. Mingled shouts from children playing ball come echoing down the streets as they play round the old gas lamp. Two women were standing at the gate of their neighbour bragging about their new coat or pair of shoes or talking about their families or the doings of their neighbours. Most of the children usually crowded round the old lamppost at the end of the street playing or talking about television. It is a dirty but merry street and no proper road only coke and dirt. Black soot is caked to the bricks and wispy smoke comes from the square chimney pots. The grumpy old men wearily sit down in the scraggy gardens talking of their younger days. The dustbins were in an awful condition but nobody cared. The street was never empty.*

There is a wealth of material for talk, for paint or clay, for dramatization and for dance drama. People are so interesting, their faces, their movements and habits communicate to us something of their lives.

AN OLD LADY I KNOW

. . . She is 92 just after Christmas, but even though she's very old she still can have a bit of fun and she's very rarely sad.

Weddy's fingers have grown so much that she has not nails because her fingers have overlapped them.

Her face is wizened and wrinkled and she's nearly deaf. Her mouth is like a round O and when she's finished speaking her mouth seems to twitch. . . .

Weddy is a very nice person and very friendly, and I shall be very sad when she dies.†

The children we are considering in this study may not yet be able to write like this, but they can talk, draw and paint, model, dance, and act.

They must travel further away from home too, so that experiences grow richer. They need to really see and be in the railway station and the castle, to be by the river and the sea, to go to the top of the hill. They need not often go far away, but a bus journey, short train journey or a walk are experiences which should come frequently.

Nature provides us with great excitement and variations. Changing weather can enchant and inspire with its variety of mood, colour, shapes, textures, and noises. No district is long without its drama. There are weddings, fires, demolition, new

* A. B. Clegg (Ed.), *The Excitement of Writing*, p. 35.
† *Ibid.*, p. 41.

buildings rising. There are festivals, special moments and events.

The teacher must be a person for whom life's materials and happenings hold a childlike enchantment. Here are the stimuli for all kinds of sensory experiences, for imaginative growth, expressiveness, and creativity, at any level. The stimulus must be as far as is possible, used as soon as it is experienced. These children cannot afford to save an experience until there is a convenient time. There must be talk and activity whilst the experience is fresh, bright and urgent.

> He is the Headmaster of a secondary school in a Fifeshire mining town and has obtained remarkable results with not over endowed pupils by taking them out in small groups to a hut in the hills, and bringing to life a variety of subjects—social, botanical, geological—which were dull or meaningless in the schoolroom.*

This head brought to life botany, geology, and geography. For the poor learner we must use all experiences, the simple, obvious things as well as the unusual and more exotic, to provide food for language and for understanding.

* Chaim Bermant reviewing *Escape from the Classroom* by R. F. Mackenzie, *The Observer*, November 1965.

CHAPTER 12

THE ARTS AS COMMUNICATION

We cannot fathom the mystery of a single flower, nor is it intended that we should, but that the pursuit of science should constantly be stayed by the love of beauty, and accuracy of knowledge by tenderness of emotion. Nor is it even just to speak of the love of beauty as in all respects unscientific, for there is a science of the aspects of things as well as of their nature, and it is as much a fact to be noted in their constitution that they produce such and such an effect upon the eye or heart (as for instance, that minor scales of sound cause melancholy) as that they are made up of certain atoms or vibrations of matter.*

In writing of the arts which are obviously the ones which all children can use to communicate, and which these particular children need so badly, I attempt only to emphasize those points about each art which seem to be most relevant in this context, considering the educational channels necessary and possible for these special children. I am not attempting to analyse fully the teaching approach and the material available in each medium. This extensive work is well done in some cases elsewhere and in any case is not the province of this book.

We are concerned with the personal development of children and at all levels learning and experience involve many and interlocking tracts and adventures. The arts in particular are interwoven and are discussed under individual headings only for clarity and convenience. "There is close relation between the art and life at every point. Like the colours of a rainbow one art merges into another almost imperceptibly. Everything is interrelated."†

* John Ruskin, *Modern Painters*, vol. 3, p. 325.
† M. Petrie, *Art and Regeneration*, p. 44.

The Visual Arts

Teachers do find it relatively easy to give children the opportunity to draw, paint, and to make things with materials. The facility with which most children do this, however inadequately from adult points of view, means that if a teacher supplies only material, opportunity, and the slightest stimulus, children can obtain release, enjoyment, and can to some extent express themselves. There is scope through the use of materials for communication at all levels, from the earliest scrubbing action and scribbles of the nursery child and of some children who though much older are still at this stage of exploring, to the ordered expression of shape and form which one tends to expect from the older pupil who has gained greater skill of hand and eye and has developing perception and needs.

Difficulties arise in that a teacher often does not know how to enrich the stimulus, how to help children to become observant about that which is around them, and to encourage that curiosity and liveliness of vision which is the gift of most children. He may not have the sensitivity to know when to leave a child to his own exploring and creating with material, or how to help as the need for greater skill arises. He may not himself be stimulated by or be knowledgeable enough about materials which can be exciting and useful to the child at a particular stage reached. He may not himself be awakened to the world of shape, form, and texture. This is not condemnation of such a teacher. Education is an urgent business as it is interpreted in school today, and many things have to be "taught". As many teachers see the situation, time spent in drawing, painting, exploring, and making with clay, sawing, and carving, might well be spent in what for some children is further struggle with the skills of reading and number, which the teacher particularly of the least able children sees as being ever more urgent. Art takes so much time. A great deal of mess and untidiness takes place, money is spent, and lovely clean paper is "messed up". Trouble and energy are involved: there are materials to order and to store, to arrange and to collect, and one knows that there is the possibility of little tangible result at first with the less able children. One needs to be a teacher who believes that this is a worth-while channel for him to follow, that it is not a time-spending way of happily occupying, but that results will be at best inner ones and that here is a learning channel. The ability to read and write is indeed urgent for these children, but the ways are not often direct ones.

I speak of course only generally. There have been and are great educators who have established respectability for the visual arts in education, and many serving teachers enthusiastically teach art in a very lively way, even though it is not their personal great love, not that there shall be, "The training of the hand to execute with nicety and precision and the eye to discern degrees of variation in the straight lines from the perpendicular or horizontal,"* but that art should be a force in the development of a child from his earliest years.

The visual arts are at least tangible to the average teacher. He is able to set about the task. It may not progress very far educationally, but in most schools for children with learning difficulties some time is spent with crayon, paint, needlework, woodwork, and simple crafts using cardboard, and other waste materials. Too often these crafts are repetitive ones such as knitting, rug making, and embroidery on marked material, where the child is, it is true, gaining a certain satisfaction in the moderate success of so producing an article, perhaps acquiring some dexterity of fingers and standard of neatness and persistence in a task, but is spending so much time which could be used creatively, enlivening, and feeding starved imagination. Teachers are so afraid of accepting a child's creative work and feel somehow shame for what is produced creatively by these children, a necessity to touch it up or to do the important part, yet at the same time expressing emphatically that "they cannot do much".

In few schools and special classes is this aspect of the arts looked

* Quoted from a circular on the teaching of drawing to infant boys from the Board of Education to Her Majesty's Inspectors, 1890, in *Ten Years of Change*, West Riding Education Committee, 1953, p. 52.

upon as a major educative force. Rather, once established, it is play time for the child, restful for the teacher, a relief between or after bouts of struggle with "more serious things". It takes a rather more prominent place as such than drama, dance, or music.

Many teachers doubt the ability of the child who does not succeed in the basic educational skills to succeed in any art. "They have no imagination." "They cannot handle things." "They do pattern but not much else." These are the kinds of remarks which I have heard many times. It is true, of course, that many difficulties beset these children in the handling of tools and in organizing that which they wish to express. There is poverty often of food for expression, yet here there is much greater freedom of language for them to use than in that of the written word, and one does so often come across unsuspected vitality of expression, even detail and obvious understanding from a child who expresses through his painting, drawing, and modelling. These children do often enjoy and persist in pattern making and there is the need for stimulation which urges them to other fields of creative activity with paint and clay, but we must remember that design is for them particularly valuable. There is security and satisfaction of order, and the necessary growth of flow, rhythm, and spatial sense. There is not enough attempt to offer a rich field so that every child stands a chance of being stimulated and satisfied. Teachers have special preferences for materials and subjects and tend to look little further or to be unaware that they are limiting the children. So one does sometimes find a marked accent on boats, trains, and bridges in a class taught by a man, and on flowers, countryside, and people in a class taught by a woman, indicating perhaps that the teacher's preferences are too strong or are making too major a contribution over too long a time.

Not many special schools or classes are using materials with anything approaching the versatility and richness which one finds in many good infant schools. The children are much more exploring their surroundings and their work which links up with these visits does involve modelling and drawing, but there is not enough art for its own sake, where the children have great freedom to express and are not immediately setting out to make a display.

Yet here surely is a language through which communication can take place for these children at their own level of development. "From within man has come his relationship with the outer world in the form which we know as art."*

If a teacher insists that this particular child senses no world around him, then that world must be enriched and enlarged so that he does. By using materials with which to express he comes to know and understand, to assess the nature of plants, animals, people, and things, to see how light falls and how colour changes. A child certainly will paint what he knows or imagines, but in doing so he comes to know more, about shape, distance, structure, and relationships.

It is important that teachers allow the children to explore the nature of materials, to express in abstract and symbolic form, and do not expect children's creative work to conform to their own ideas of beauty or rightness. They should not ask, "What is it?" or show the child "How to do it", but learn to wait and be prepared for anything with ready appreciation.

There is the two-way activity of taking in and giving out. It is the teacher's task to help children become more aware of and more interested in nature, the man-made world, and everything around, both inside and out, in things and places to be reached by such travel as is possible and by bringing in to them objects and ideas. The Castle School, Castleford, have in their hall a constantly kept and renewed display corner in which children arrange materials, flowers, and objects, with care, consideration, and individuality, for their own pleasure and that of all passers by. Some schools take time and care to encourage this kind of accent upon things of beauty and interest and allow the children to be in charge.

There should be things to touch as well as things to see; stone, wood, velvet, wool, wire mesh, glass. Museum departments lend

* C. Burland, *Man and Art,* p. 11.

objects of marked interest and loveliness, fostering in children also the need for intense care of such treasures. Children collect things which they find fascinating and wish to share; queerly shaped stone, pieces of old tree branches, leaves, roots, shells, and flowers. Teachers can also collect, use photographs and projected slides and films. Some authorities have a picture and film loan service. Television programmes are often of great interest and quality. Magazines and colour supplements are full these days of interesting material. Design of pictures and books around must be stimulating and of good quality in colour and production. The teacher's writing and drawing on the board, his taste in things, and especially in clothes are all important.

That which the children express in their art will relate to their experiences of life around, stimulated by sensitive and lively teachers. They may express their deeply felt fears, angers, hopes, and loves, and through making visible their ideas come to greater harmony with them. They will gain inner direction and control as well as something of the discipline of identity with materials. "The function of art is to turn the abstract into the concrete and the concrete into the abstract."*

If a child cannot write about his thoughts, express his subconscious ideas or his conscious experiences in word language, he may dance, act, and he may draw, paint, or model. Through their expressive work in these fields we may discover something of a child's difficulties, worries, and longings, and can estimate somewhat their missing experiences and the limitations of their environment. "You have no difficulty in finding words to explain the most complicated machine and yet words seem to be futile to describe a simple taste experience."†

These children need as much freedom of time as is possible for their creative work. They must not be unnecessarily frustrated by the end of a "lesson" and the need to stop and clear up. This may present a little more trouble for the teacher, but whenever possible it must be that within reasonable limits of everyday

* H. B. Dunkel, *Whitehead on Education*, p. 126.
† E. Fromm, *Symbolic Language*, p. 20.

living a child is allowed to continue his work until the inspiration and concentration ebbs away. Concentration is often difficult for such children and the absorption which materials demand and inspire is valuable to them.

They need also exceptional freedom of space so that materials can be unjostled by others and are spread sufficiently to save accidents which frustrate so devastatingly. Not only do they need space in this sense. They need to experience and to live with, in order to grasp, an awareness of the space around them. Sensibility to space, shape, and form, and of the identity of the human body with the space around it, is in danger of being lost in the Western world. These particular children for many reasons often lack special understanding and awareness, and in the visual arts, in dance, and drama they could discover and assimilate this.

Many of these children need particularly to work alone, to have a piece of territory which is their individual working place. Sharing tables, paints, implements, and work may be social and community training which has great value when the children are ready, but in early stages it is not a fruitful plan to stress or make it necessary. This is yet another task a teacher must accept—that of being especially aware of ability of particular children to tolerate sharing. It is a responsibility which is likely to continue even when children in these groups are old enough in reasonably normal circumstances to share easily and readily. The stage of individual ownership, of territory, and material may for many reasons still persist.

They need materials in rich supply and of such quality that work is facilitated rather than hindered. Paper should be generous in size and thick enough to hold paint well, paint which they can mix, thick and rich in colour. Crayons, pencils, and charcoal should be strong and bold when applied. How often we see the less able children with limited, poor quality materials. The little amount of money saved is paltry in our affluent society. There will be waste only until the children can learn to love material and this they will do if the material is worth the loving.

A teacher must be ready to provide materials as she sees them to be appropriate, to give the right amount of choice so that the individual child can be discriminating without becoming confused and disordered. There must be a sensitive and timely balance between the new stimuli given and the security of repetition. A teacher, knowing her children intimately, will be aware of the need to allow a child to continue to work in a particular medium or in a particular way and when to urge change and new effort. As many of these children find comfort and security in pattern work and in craft work which has a repetitive factor, it may need a careful and skilful teacher to urge a child to another kind of activity, especially when repetitive activities seem to make such a child happy and well occupied and quiet.

Clay and other materials which the children can handle directly bring about increased tactile stimulation and sensitivity and provide a very satisfying and personal relationship. Children can handle such materials, clay, wood, paper, and paint with their fingers, and really manipulate and become acquainted with them.

Materials of all kinds are useful and important, and among communicative arts one must include the kind of needlework and embroidery which does allow the children to use materials and textures creatively. Some children will especially enjoy making and dressing dolls of all kinds, making and dressing puppets which they can use, and using fabrics which can be so fascinating creatively these days.

Bigger projects may take place as the teacher and children progress in confidence. They can make bigger paintings, murals, and friezes. There will be the need for decoration for Christmas and for special occasions, flower decoration for the classroom, dining room and for the school in general.

The activity which consistently brings enjoyment and a sense of purpose to boys in special schools and classes is woodwork. It is usually taught by a man who has a genuine love of his material and even though the activity is often routine and does not allow of much individuality, there is a good deal of satisfaction centred upon the woodwork shop. If children could really use wood, to carve, to shape, as well as to construct, the joy in the shaping of this material would be doubly valuable.

Surprisingly less often, there is great purpose and satisfaction for girls in the activities of cooking and housecraft. One does learn, sadly sometimes from a housecraft teacher that these girls cannot be trusted to do much, and must tidy the cupboards or do routine tasks. An episode which describes so vividly the absolute lack of understanding of a teacher for these children is that of the shepherd's pie which had been made by the remedial stream. The coveted, joyous, final task of putting the pattern on the top was taken over by the specialist domestic science teacher. Cooking and housecraft, close to the hearts of most girls, could so well be creative, so that cooking becomes an art, however simple the making, and learning the ingredients of homemaking, a part of this whole expressive and lively education for which I am pleading.

It is necessary for the teacher of the special child to be a special teacher. He must love materials and take the trouble to find out more about their natures and possibilities. Teachers tend to gather in a number of tricks or ideas which enable them to take the next few "art classes". So often these are "blind alleys", and having blown the paint through a milk straw, and admired the shapes it made, a new idea has to be arranged for the next lesson. It is true that these very able teachers of educationally subnormal children will have to have many good ideas, but first and foremost in this context they must have a lively interest in things which might concern their children, and a love of shape, form, and texture which invades everything done in the classroom and out of it with the children. They must have a sense of order and an ability to organize, yet not be so loving of order that exploration cannot take place.

They must be alive to the opportunities which arise in movement and dance for using and experiencing materials, as when one moves in or with muslin, net, or silk. I remember the excitement, joy, and sensitivity which arose when children experimented with dancing wearing or dragging a nylon parachute, which

I had acquired from war surplus many years ago. There will be the dramatic experience necessitating making costume and scenery, as there will be the materials used to decorate the body, and the painting and modelling which leads to drama. Teachers must be conveners of talk about things made, things seen, and ideas for future making. They must have a conception of art as a major educative force, educating and disciplining the emotions, feeding the senses, capable of calming and exciting, and fulfilling a social function.

This is a way in which these children can experience and understand. As Grözinger says, "The aim of the child's apparent artistic development is not art but reality."* A child cannot always give words to that which he has discovered, he may not even be aware of what he has discovered, but in this way he can speak. "If people learn to make pots for holding water, eventually they learn to make them beautiful, there is no language without its poetry."†

Movement, Dance, and Dance Drama

"We know more than we can say,"‡ said Whitehead.

How true this is of many of the children we are considering. Word language is for them a barrier to communication and if communication remains blocked, the language of words, so much the link to thought, cannot grow.

> The commonest fact about all of us is that each has a living body, the whole of our culture springs from the movements of our bodies. . . . "Mind" remains an abstraction unless we can describe it by the language of the body. We could see nothing, say nothing, do nothing, and think nothing.**

By movement I am not first considering the acquisition of skills recognized in athletics, games, and sports, but the use of the human body to express in gesture, in dance-like movement play, in dance, and dance drama. Through bodily movement a

* W. Grözinger, *Scribbling, Drawing and Painting*, p. 20.
† G. Lisitzley, *Four Ways of being Human*, p. 19.
‡ H. B. Dunkel, *Whitehead on Education*, p. 26.
** P. Meredith, *Mind and Movement*, 1963.

person expresses most directly and most simply his ideas and needs, yet in schools for children who find communication difficult there is very little opportunity for them to express in this way. One finds rather the ordered country dance in which once more the child must learn a pattern set from outside and once again his expressive outlet is severely limited. It is perhaps because in movement and dance so much arises from the child himself, because dance can allow for the individual to express in his own way, that teachers find the work so frightening. There seem to be few pegs upon which they can hang, few border lines or measurements, and a teacher has doubts about an activity seemingly so loosely structured. This is not so, of course, but one must have understanding of movement and a creative attitude towards teaching. Yet for a child who is failing in recognized skills, here is an activity where there are no outside obstacles, no competition, no rigid right or wrong. He can come to move more quickly or more smoothly than he could before, to go lower or higher, to jump with greater resilience, to transfer easily from one kind of movement to another, but what he does can be his own, coming from his inner feelings, thought and effort and leaving with him an experience of his own doing.

Movement is the most fundamental of all languages. It speaks from the whole person. The ingredients of the movement language can be expressed in words, but they are such that a rich word vocabulary is required. Movements have infinite tones and shades and each person's gestures are unique to him. We often inspire children's movement using words and they can describe their actions in words. All the time the word language grows through real experience—softly, quickly, smoothly, round, sharp, twisted; shrinking, stretching, curling, rushing, falling, jumping. If one were aiming mainly to teach words, the activity would be more than worth while, but here is a language through which these children can already communicate. From their own stage of development they can become involved, "speaking out" with their bodies. Movement involves feeling, the senses are awakened, particularly the kinaesthetic awareness which remains so often undeveloped. The body may be inco-ordinate, especially where there is an impairment involving body control. How much more then should we use the body to help awareness and sensitivity. It is a fact that when a class of educationally subnormal children has been involved in movement and dance there has been little evidence of subnormality. The difficulties of balance and speed of response in some cases are far outweighed by the absorption and sensitivity which the children show.

Children all need to be brought to an awareness of body image and space relationship. This awareness of body is neglected in education, even in physical education, dance, and drama. For these children especially one must give greater sensitivity, knowledge, and confidence of body. They do so often lack an awareness of three dimensions and through movement the focusing of their consciousness upon the space around them through which the parts of the human body pass in gesture, and in moving shapes, one can increase this sensitivity and understanding. In conjunction with modelling and an awareness of shape and form, one can awaken the whole world of three-dimensional consciousness for them. "Dance is fluid sculpture. Dance retains something of the statuesque, a plastic art."* Through movement and dance one may excite and awaken, or calm and quieten. One can bring about the awareness of strength and vitality in the body, delicacy, and the feeling and experience of lightness and of the air around. The qualities of movement are those of the living world— quickness, sustainment, and all the degrees of the speed of moving things, deviousness and twistedness, directness and arrow-like sharpness, strength and vigour, tenderness and delicacy. The human body has a rich vocabulary in strength, time, and space. Through movement children can come to relate to other people— sharing the floor space, sharing the idea, making physical contact, moving in a partnership or in a group.

Through movement the child comes to awareness of rhythm, a rhythm involving his whole self. He becomes aware of pauses and stillnesses, of going and stopping, of movements which flow

* V. G. Aldrich, *Philosophy of Art*, p. 67.

on into one another. So often these particular children have great need of harmony in their rhythmic lives. Many have never been able to establish their own rhythms whilst struggling with those of the outside world which did not seem to fit. With the assistance of conscious movement phrases, of repetition, of success and pleasure, the rhythm of life might become more established, less erratic, and more conducive to emotional and personal growth. These children may come through movement to a realisation of self, to a self-confidence which allows them to communicate in other ways.

It is with great confidence that I write of this art as the one through which the educationally failing child might well come to a greater state of learning readiness. It is an art in the centre of all arts, linking with rhythm, sound, shape and form, texture, nature, people, and the happenings of life.

There is one great difficulty—the scarcity of teachers who having absorbed deeply knowledge of human movement and the ways in which one might stimulate a full development in others, have the love and sensitivity to bring it to these particular children. There should be little difficulty once teachers realize the urgency and need, because the children are, in my experience, first eager to please, and then delighted and entranced by their own experiences. As a teacher one can use a rich vocabulary to communicate ideas to the children. One can at least be aware if children cannot understand the words used. There are other forms of communication too, one can use sound, music, pictures, the garden, a walk in the town, or even movement!

Patrick Meredith, in his article "Mind and movement", says:

> Several years ago at a school in Yorkshire I witnessed something of the educational impact of Laban's ideas. What it demonstrated was that by starting from the movement of the child's own body the whole educational behaviour of the child, including, reading, writing and drawing, could be freed, energized and evicted in ways which have to be seen to be believed.

This is not the place to expound at length the study of human movement for which we are so indebted to Rudolph Laban. This is done so well in other writing and in his own: there are many of Laban's pupils teaching today in schools and colleges in Britain and in various parts of the world, and his teaching is vigorously and faithfully perpetuated at the Laban Art of Movement Centre at Addlestone, Surrey. Education owes a great debt of gratitude to this great man who has helped us to understand movement as human expressiveness and has enabled us as teachers therefore, to be clear enough in our understanding so that children may consciously use their movement capacities to explore and exploit in order to communicate fully in this medium.

Movement is the ingredient of dance as words are the ingredients of poetry. Douglas Kennedy said:

> All mobile organisms dance where they are in a state of high activity.
> Among primitives, children and uncivilized tribes, there is a close rela-
> tion between a rhythmical motion and the emotion or feeling of elation
> that it induces. If a primitive feels joy and dances because of the feelings
> he can subsequently induce that joy by repeating the joy dance. This
> spontaneous action and reaction between the feeling inside and the ex-
> pression "outside", of a rhythmic gesture is normal to most children, but
> not to most grown ups—normal to most primitive races, but not to civilized
> ones.*

This relationship and interaction between the inner self and the outward expression is a factor which is most profoundly important in education. How wrong is the physical educationalist who writes:

> Some girls claimed they would like to have lessons in deportment, al-
> though it is doubtful if they have any conception of the tedium involved in
> obtaining and maintaining a graceful carriage.†

Grace and deportment are not won tediously. They are the emerging of personal quality, growing from within. Moments when a child dances, when movement is filled with feeling and meaning happen quite naturally with the help of a teacher who guides the way to a richer and fuller vocabulary of movement and urges form and rhythmic shape to clarify communication. A child skips along the street, jumps into the air, swirls

* D. Kennedy, Lecture, *The Origin of Dance Expression*, April 1955.
† Some views on P.E. programmes, *Physical Education*, vol. 58, no. 174.

around and around in sheer joy, expressed most fundamentally.

Guided by a teacher the language can be exploited, controlled, and disciplined so that instead of "speaking" in movements like isolated words or shouts, a child can speak in movement sentences, phrases where accents emerge, and parts become less or more important. A dance phrase has a beginning, a middle content, and a clear end in its simplest form, and so communication becomes clear, firm, and confident. Children dance so much with their whole being that their absorption is deeply engrossing. Here is the concentration of first-class learning and a discipline which must be primarily individual and ultimately self imposed.

Such movement involves intensely the rhythmic "vibration". "On such an animated vibrant creature the pulsation of sound rhythm or sight (gesture) rhythm falls with immediate effect."*

The rhythm may be inside, silent but visible in the shaping and timing of gesture. Children soon find sound and movement to be close partners, and dance accompanies or is accompanied by vocal sound, percussion, words, or music. The relationship between sound and music and the dance must be fully discussed in the section on music. There is a great link here; these two important communicating forces join together so easily and often advantageously whilst each, dance and music, can be without each other.

When there is accompanying sound a child begins to apply his own rhythmic self, his own freedom to partner an outside discipline. Awareness and control must be summoned to accompany the communication which may have begun so freely and individually or may have been "set alight" by rhythmic sound.

Dance becomes involved with the nature of things and people around, and with ideas which arise in connection with life. This is not mime but a transfer of feelings and understanding into movement. Just as one expresses through a sigh or a shrug or an impulsive wave of the arm, the child expresses his understanding of the coming of warmth bringing movement to the frozen pond, the vitality of growth through a hardened earth in spring, the

* D. Kennedy, *op. cit.*

soft gentleness of a warm west wind, or the fast, ruthless strength of water. Qualities are absorbed from outside in, and they emerge as did the sigh or the shrug. Movement is so easily stimulated by the qualities, shapes, and relationships of that which surrounds children. They are still delighted by things which we later do not any longer notice—the shape of a stone, the skeleton of a leaf, the spider's web hanging, the way in which rain hits the ground, or the strength of tall chimneys. Children can often dance their ideas which they have gathered in and have been unable to sort out, understand, or communicate. How one realizes the immense amount which children do assimilate when one sees movement creation arising! Words have not been there to express but the movement language is less remote and can communicate so much more fully for them than words. They dance with movements of animals, they shape their bodies as the sharp rocks of the sea-shore, they can be inspired by all that is around in nature and the man-made world.

Dance drama, like narrative poetry, plays with the idea, extends it, and enjoys the licence taken. A dancer becomes transformed in movement fantasy. Here a child with little confidence can live for a while within another world, absorbed and secure, and can clarify and express.

A teacher can help this process of communication by bringing through her teaching an increasing consciousness of movement language and by helping children to "speak" clearly in movement, to "speak out" in space with confidence, and by constantly enriching the movement language through full use of bodily parts, of space, of quality, and effort, so that each individual becomes a richer mover with extended uniqueness. Children will all have their own movement characteristics, but all can become more able to use qualities which they find difficult and to enhance those which come most easily. A child may find it natural to move with sparkling quickness but more difficult to go smoothly. He may enjoy soft, delicate gesture and stepping, but have to acquire the ability to use vigour and strength. In this area of development, a teacher has an important part to play.

While the movement language grows, as with the acquisition of words, communication becomes fuller and more free. This is a steadily mounting process; expression and communication bring stimulus for further exploration and discovery.

My interest in the education of children in special classes and in schools for the educationally subnormal children first arose whilst teaching dance and dance drama to these children. Their response startled teachers and others with considerable experience in this field. Once the children had become used to me as a person, and when I had ascertained their speed of response, it was relatively simple to find ways of imparting stimulating ideas and help with movement language and the framework for creating phrases, sequences, and dances. Almost always words could be found which suited the needs of most of them, and these, augmented as is natural when one is absorbed by bodily attitude, small gesture, and vocal quality were enough for all. Communication between us was usually easy and free. It seemed sometimes to be advantageous to use extra stimuli. For instance, we took a walk through the autumn leaves on a windy day and I brought a picture of the rolling ocean, far out in the Pacific where most of us could not have been. We often used percussive sound and music to help our movement ideas and as stimuli for dance. This language was easily shared and most fundamentally understood.

It is impossible to discuss simply the particular difficulties which educationally subnormal children encounter in this kind of expressive activity because the range and variation of handicap is so great, but it is possible to indicate areas where there could easily be need for especial care in approach, for accent or delay. Many of these children are excitable and easily aroused to a state of lack of control and over-tension. This is often the source of behaviour problems when a teacher finds the children impossible to control. They are very susceptible to atmosphere. Unusual weather, an unexpected event, pending or past, or the mood of a single child, can mean that a movement class has to be especially carefully handled. In any case there is a special need for a secure framework, for a quiet, steady voice and approach, for a pattern which is established and remains intact for long enough to give a sense of security, so that energy may be reserved for the content of the lesson. I found when teaching a large, excitable class where calm and quiet were very necessary for the children, that for a time it was best to establish that they relaxed on the floor, shutting the eyes when they were ready with their shoes changed or off, whilst quiet, melodic music played. This meant that when the music was finished, when the last note had died away and I had softly turned the record player off, I could speak quietly and smoothly and we could begin to move and to become absorbed in what we did. Soon I was usually able to enliven and stimulate their movement without their losing control or concentration.

Very often these children have too great a measure of tension. Their movement is often bound in flow and there is a lack of ability to open out. These difficulties must be dealt with patiently and slowly. They derive from fear and insecurity and cannot immediately be thrown off. Everything that brings confidence— rhythm, sound, praise, encouragement, guidance, and the use of fantasy—must be at the teacher's finger tips so that such tension can gradually be overcome.

Some children in these classes are especially over-relaxed and over-free, they tend to heaviness, and their movement lacks resilience and clarity. These children need clear framework for their movement phrases, strong rhythms, lively sound accompaniment, and clear body positions in pauses, beginnings, and ends of movements. Stillness is especially important. There must be moments when the body is completely controlled, when there can be awareness of body position. Stillness when attention is turned inwards upon the self brings about quiet concentration which the teacher can use for the next effort.

These children, like any other people, have individual difficulties of extreme slowness or haste, heaviness, over-tension, or over-lightness, vagueness in use of space, or an over-economic, erratic, or jerky gesture pattern. Their difficulties tend to be extreme. Slow movers tend to be very slow; the over-active, very much so. Bodily handicaps for some children further complicate their efforts to express. The hemiplegic child has obvious one-sided bodily difficulty and a greatly impaired total balance, the brain-damaged child often has difficulty in co-ordination. Many children have minor physical defects. The partially sighted child may find balance extremely difficult. Sometimes children, especially those suffering from epilepsy, are under sedation, and a teacher must be very aware that she is not attempting to force the child against this. A teacher in a special school must, in particular, know the children's movement capacities intimately so that she is acutely aware of individual difficulties and factors about which she should take care. The child with hearing disability may not only have difficulty in following advice and lesson pattern, but may have intolerance to some percussive and musical sounds. The overweight child may be slow and inco-ordinate, and it is not very helpful to point this out to her. He or she may become breathless at the least exertion. There may be acute self-conscious-ness about movement or about changing into freer clothes for the lesson. A teacher must be particularly alive to the moment when concentration begins to lessen. The length of time during which these children can really remain absorbed varies from day to day and interest is easily broken by minor disturbance.

Finally, I must mention the slight difficulty of communication from teacher to child. It is a small matter, because the teacher will be aware of the main word vocabulary known to most of the children and should try all the time to express herself richly in language, body attitude, and gesture, and with any other aids she feels right and necessary or useful, being always ready to abandon ideas and to try again.

There are, however, many factors which those who teach movement, dance, and dance drama to these children will find especially satisfying and some respects in which it is an easier process than that of teaching children who succeed so much more easily in more accepted school tasks. There is in the work with these children a simplicity which reminds one of the words spoken by Martha Grahame during her film *A Dancer's World*, when she says about dance, "What you do you do for the first time".

There is for the children who have found so little success so much less fear that they will "look silly". They become more easily absorbed and give to their dance a sense of intense happiness in play. They do not find the need for complicated solutions to problems and there is usually great sincerity and honesty in expression.

A bottom stream class in a girls' secondary school where dance has taken a prominent place for some time on the time-table wrote about these lessons. Their writing was executed with difficulty, but many expressed the release and happiness which dance obviously brought to them.

> I forget about the other lessons.
>
> It is a lot of fun.
>
> A change from sitting in desks.
>
> I express my feelings.
>
> It gets your mind off things.
>
> You are free.
>
> I like it sad, then gay.
>
> It makes you feel fresh and open.
>
> I am really happy when I am dancing, it has got a feeling like spring even if I am dancing in winter.*

For these children fantasy is release, enrichment for the imagination, and a way to creativity. Through fantasy they can come to terms with their fears, hopes, and thoughts. They are often much less inhibited imaginatively than children from the academically able classes. This has been my experience over a period of many years. One works very hard sometimes to urge an A class to freedom from self-consciousness and to expressiveness. It would seem that just as the educational process has the effect of destroying imaginative quality, so it is destroyed more surely in the classes where children are urged on to more and more memorizing and the acquisition of more and more skills, where the pace is competitive, and progress is measured in terms of marks gained and a place attained ahead of others.

* Girls from Mary Linwood School, Leicester, 1961.

Bodily the children of little apparent learning ability become through this kind of movement and dance, confident, and poised. These qualities last at least while the children are participating. For this reason it has been with astonishment sometimes that those few people observing such classes have later discovered that they were "special" or "E". Some children in schools where the accent is upon expressive life and personality growth, have this quality for much longer, at least during the school day, and one knows that the drooping, hang-dog appearance and the dull look which so often characterize children in this category are not necessary. There can be increased awareness which helps the head to lift, and gives alertness to the whole body. There is also the result of increased metabolic aliveness, circulatory stimulus, and nervous awakening, the whole being becoming more fully aroused, more sensitive, more tonic. It is in this lesson, well conducted, that eyes can really begin to shine.

Drama

> Drama has a double psychological function. It acts as a release of phantasy and also as a means of grasping reality. Both aspects are equally important and finally interdependent.*

A dictionary definition of dramatic includes the words "vivid", "thrilling", and "emotionally stirring". Drama includes the whole world of activity which involves "becoming" or portraying another person, or being in an imagined situation. For children, this dramatic activity most often fully involves them in "becoming" someone or something other than themselves. A child loses his identity within a character and becomes transformed. Dramatic activity in school should be "vivid", "thrilling", and "emotionally stirring". This does not mean that it is only the shooting down of gangsters or the crashing of an aeroplane. The undisturbed dramatic play of very young children is often quiet and homely; they become mother, and father, the doctor, and the nurse, and patients in the hospital, but such play is fully

* M. Hourd, *Education of the Poetic Spirit*, p. 63.

undertaken and children are usually vividly involved. When drama is used as an expressive activity in school, material does need to be transporting, removed far enough from everyday life to provide for the children dramatic situations.

What kinds of activities come under this heading for children? There is a close link with dance and often it is hard to decide whether children dance or act. Imagination emerges symbolically or more realistically and expression is through movement. In a hall, at the same time, in a similarly stimulated situation, there may be children dancing and children acting. The action may be mimetic, portraying as nearly as possible the actual movements, exaggerated somewhat to make up for lack of words or sounds, and perhaps the lack of properties. In my experience most children find expressing through movement, whether it be mime or dance or dance drama, an easier language than that of the spoken word, but for children who have difficulties with word language and for many who have speech difficulties, it is a very much more ready vehicle for dramatic expression, and whilst it is obviously important that words shall be used as soon as is possible in their dramatic activity, it is wise to allow confidence to develop without words. Through movement those children can gain security, immersed in their fantasy, and safe in the person and situation of their imagination. Demanding or even encouraging words too early is so often a cause of lack of absorption. The dramatic situation is no longer present when the teacher asks, "What do you think you would say?"—then—"Well, hurry up". A long silence follows while the child struggles for words and the flow and imagination for all are gone. If teachers encourage any vocal sound that arises, a grunt, a sigh, an exclamation, words will eventually come. Certainly one would never prevent this, but rather greet such a venture with the greatest encouragement.

Free, improvised dramatic play arises naturally as infant children play in the Wendy House or on the lawn, or as boys in infant and junior schools act out the "Western" in the playground. Teachers can learn much about the powers of absorption and imagination of the child from watching this kind of activity arise, stimulated by articles from the dressing-up box, by the builder's materials left in the yard, a story recently told, or a popular television programme.

For the less able children, help is needed often so that they have the confidence even to play in this way. Stimulation can be provided through stories told, experiences given, and the provision of exciting spaces, corners in the playground and garden, tree trunks and dens, alcoves, and freely arranged classrooms. Teachers have the obligation to help further by the sponsoring of drama as an activity, recognized and respected in the school programme. This is important for all children, but especially so for the children we are discussing.

It is necessary to put a framework around the activity within which imagination can be set free. Always this framework must leave freedom for each individual to give of himself. It is so where all expressive activity in education is concerned. In drama this framework is sometimes difficult for the teacher to define. It must be a flexible framework, particularly so here, the teacher always being ready to tighten or to enlarge as the needs of the children become apparent.

A teacher might introduce the idea, helping the children's imagination to become awakened. He might suggest ideas which all can try. He will be responsible for the starts and the pauses. He may sponsor the shape of the drama, giving the children an outline pattern of space and action, so that within this they may create. This sponsoring of the framework is so often a task which a teacher fails to do adequately, particularly with less able and less confident children. Drama can involve many people and if a group of people are to react to one another there must be an outline pattern within which action takes place, because they are learning how to communicate clearly. It may be that the teacher plans the hall. "This is the forest. Here is the path which leads up the mountain." The size of the framework depends upon the experience of the children and the complexity of the action. Never will it be so small and tight that the children's own imagination is stifled, yet it must not be so large that children are bewildered and lost. So often one sees dramatic activity where the teacher is trying to give freedon for the children to express, but there is not enough guidance and only a disheartening confusion arises, an end being an abrupt intervention by an angry teacher who is then more convinced that these children cannot use this kind of activity.

Drama for these special children has a particular part to play. Describing drama at his school, a headmaster says:

> Drama at Turner's Court is considered as something more than merely acting. The whole importance lies in its therapeutic value. . . . increased self-confidence, a lessening of tension, an awareness of other people's feelings, an appreciation of deportment and speech, a desire to learn, or simply the ability to laugh at himself.*

This headmaster is very aware of the unpredictable quality of creative activity for these or indeed for any children. Children gain from their participation in different things, but whatever they gain there will be little that is negative and much that is immensely valuable.

One important factor lies in the power drama has of transporting one from the real life situation. The burden which some of these children bear of being themselves, the person who does not do well, is not very clever, not very popular, or goes home each day to a drab home, can be lifted for a while when they become the king, the teacher, the sailor, the mother, or even the burglar. The intensity with which the lethargic, dull-eyed child can become transformed is startling, even alarming in the vividness which reveals necessity. Much-needed absorption and concentration are attained, imagination grows, and through such activity children gain release and understanding.

Speech, as we have seen, is very important for these children. As happens when some children sing, the flow of words previously and in everyday life so bound up, sometimes miraculously becomes freer within this imaginative spell.

For these children particularly, freedom of speech and, of course, of gesture, is desirable in their drama. They may appear

* R. P. Menday and J. Wiles, *The Everlasting Childhood*, p. 185.

to find security in the set play, but the quality of imagination will suffer from the effort required to learn words and to attain the stage of performing, even if it is ever acquired. Failure is possible for some children at least, and success is what we are trying to achieve.

These children sometimes do enjoy and benefit from playing with an audience present. It means that they really give something. They are proud and happy to be of use and of service. Drama is most often best left at the stage when children act for their own sake, but when children who succeed so little do dramatic work which can be shown, preferably to a child audience, this should occasionally be so. A teacher must realize, however, that when an audience is present, there is of necessity imposed upon the children an extra responsibility of communication to that audience another dimension which may disturb the dramatic quality previously attained. This performance will have for the children another function, that of giving, of sharing. Too often the dramatic activity of the special class or school is put on for parents and friends with all good will, perhaps to raise money for extra things in school, or as a thank offering to generous friends, but people watch in amused surprise that these children can manage this.

Drama for these children is an activity of learning, involving them deeply and intimately, and establishing for them relationships which in everyday life are not easy to make. Material must be chosen with care. A teacher must not imagine because the children are not academically able that infant material is suitable for the older child. They must, of course, be able to comprehend and to have a desire to use ideas. Much discussion must take place, some argument, some rejection.

Costume and properties help to give security and to enliven imagination. A child feels safe in a cloak or large hat, safer still behind a mask, as a shadow behind a screen or as a puppet.

Children who are in our special category are often very easy to inspire dramatically and have vivid and fresh imaginative quality, lacking the self-consciousness of the child who has more scholastic ability. They sometimes "play" more readily and as they find that here they can succeed and are not measured against another, confidence grows and drama becomes more lively and vivid to the astonishment of teachers.

Drama needs space. It is important that for most of the time all children are involved. This is not always easy. A teacher takes perhaps some risks of disorder. There may be noise—dramatic and other noise. The hall is often not available and the space of playground or field is too large and lacks intimacy even in still, warm weather. One might find a corridor, clear the classroom, or use a corner of the garden on a still day. Like dance, drama demands very creative teaching. One cannot forecast what the events will be. Alertness and imagination are always in demand. One cannot wonder that so many teachers resort to half-hearted drama where a group acts in the front of the class, but it is worth while to try better things.

Dramatic activity in the widest sense is worth while. When children, having a movement language upon which to call, become used to a larger space, when a teacher stimulates with good, interesting material and ensures a suitable framework, children of all abilities in our schools can use drama. There will be always an aspect whereby children release and portray ideas, but more than this, children can become free, important, growing in understanding of situations, people, and words. They can learn to share and to succeed.

> The value lies in the fact that it comes from within the child and is not imposed upon him by the teacher, it releases his shyness and inhibitions instead of making him self conscious, and when well done it helps him to build up in him that private confidence in his own capacity which does so much to help him tackle the formal subjects of instruction.*

Music

NOTE OF MELANCHOLY

The recent survey of music in special schools carried out by the Schools Music Association shows a wide range of music therapy from crude

* *Ten Years of Change*, West Riding Education Committee, 1953, p. 51.

rhythm beating to appreciation of classical records—in use in only a very limited number of special schools.

More than half the schools circularized by the Schools Music Association did not reply and the impression from those who did is that a large majority have not accepted the effects of music as any more than incidentally therapeutic.*

One might reasonably be extremely critical of the place which has in the recent past been taken by music in the education of all children. Teachers of music on the whole have been slow to realize the necessity for this art to be part of every child's inheritance. There has been, and still remains, a tendency for the teacher of music to be interested only in the musical children, to tend to exclude the "growlers", to concentrate on the choir and the school orchestra. There was, for instance, the school where only the A-stream had access to recorder playing. There is much more music developing in our schools, much more instrumental playing, and intensely increased opportunities for the gifted child. Nevertheless, teachers of music are taking a long time to come to educational understanding which makes them aware of the way in which music festivals and competitions most often ignore the less able child, and use money, effort, and energy for display purposes, when the real reason for musical education is the enrichment and development in personality and in resources for communication and pleasure for all children.

Music in education has, of course, helped to bring about progress in the world of music at a high level. Children have opportunities now to develop their musical ability which they did not previously encounter and one would not wish to minimize the great importance to us all that talent and desire in music are accorded adequate opportunity. We have still to clarify for some people the place of music in education, to help educationalists understand the nature of music, and musicians the needs of education.

There are, however, many people who work consistently and with great understanding for the expansion of musical education as an educative force, and some such as Juliette Alvin who are

* Note of melancholy, *The Teacher*, 30 July 1965.

especially aware of and devote great energy to the establishment of music as a means of communication for the educationally subnormal and for other handicapped children.

Music has a difficult language which can provide a barrier for children, and indeed for others, including teachers. There are not enough teachers who have musical knowledge and not enough people with musical knowledge who can or wish to teach. Many who love music think that they could not tackle the task of teaching this art, and quite often a school is devoid even of a teacher to accompany the morning hymn. Yet here is another language which can bring so much confidence, pleasure, and learning help, to the educationally less able child.

"What does it mean?" Schumann was asked. "It means this", and Schumann played it again.*

It is sometimes thought that educationally subnormal children have exceptional musical ability. Mr. Dobbs looked carefully into this question and did not find it to be so.† It may be that the children do succeed in music to a much greater degree than they do in the skills of reading, writing, and number. Arnold Bentley does not consider musical ability and what we call intelligence to be highly correlated.‡ Music can be for these children a channel of communication more open to them than we realize until opportunity to sing, listen, make rhythm, and dance, is given.

Sometimes music can answer subconscious needs, bringing an entirely non-verbal, non-intellectual outlet, as when one dances freely and unthinking, carried by the music. There is great emotional release and satisfaction in singing, clapping, and tapping, however simple the music or elementary the pulse.

In less civilized and less industrialized and commercial communities, music, dance, and drama might well be part of life with which children are identified for their earliest years and through

* J. Todd (Ed.), *The Arts, Artists and Thinkers*, p. 138.

† J. Dobbs, The influence of music on the retarded child, M.Ed. thesis, University of Durham, 1954.

‡ A. Bentley, *Musical Ability in Children and its Measurement* .

which they become socially adjusted and successful people in a community.

Music can serve the mood, can bring expression to gaiety, aggression, or contemplation. Music can bring balance, calm to the over excited, liveliness to the lethargic, steadiness to the uncontrolled. It can transport into a world of fantasy, can help to relieve tension, and to serve imagination. The senses are awakened, not only to sound, but to all the qualities with which sounds can be related; softness, harshness, strength, delicacy, harmony, and discord. The emotions are aroused very easily for most people by music; the mind absorbs sound and begins to relate and to understand, however simply, and the body is stimulated by rhythm, stress, and flow.

This is a flexible, rich medium and it should be possible to offer children a balanced diet of music to release, to stimulate, to bring calm and relaxation, and to give them experience over a wide range of activity, imagination, and sound.

"Music seems to have an immediate communion with my life", said Coleridge.*

It is important that children become involved in music. They must make music in many ways, dance to music, and listen actively. There is so much background sound today, and "listening" can mean just being present. Volume must not be so great that they hear only noise. Listening needs effort. It is a process of giving oneself to the task of concentration, not always easy for these children, yet an exercise which they need so badly. Live music is especially good for them. Juliette Alvin plays her cello sitting close to the children. They first help her to get it from the case, are allowed to feel the bow, even to make sound with it across the strings. Children can feel the silence which precedes the first note and appreciate the wonder of that silence. They can be stimulated to real listening.

Music brings friendliness, happiness, and security, as when one sings to a baby, when a group sing or play together while sitting around, walking, or doing a monotonous task. Music can bring

* K. Coburn (Ed.), *Inquiring Spirit: A New Presentation of Coleridge*, p. 214.

sharing with others. Each child must be able to contribute at his own level and must not be faced with rejection because he sings out of tune or plays at the wrong time. By sharing music he may come more easily to sing in tune and to become rhythmically aware. Singing out of tune is not a very sure guide to unmusicality and to reject these children, apart from the harm done to those concerned, is often hasty and misguided from the musical point of view.

The withdrawn child is often drawn out through music, and sometimes music offers the first and clearest opening for communication. Achievement comes about by the singing of a new song or the playing of a new tune. It is important, as in all learning, to stretch the resources of the children, but to ensure some success. This might be done by the singing of a song already learned to precede the new effort required. They can bear some failure if it is tempered by success. Attention is very necessary for these children and through music the whole of a child's vitality can be focused, for a short time at least. So often children who find the skills of the classroom beyond them have developed long-standing habits of vague attention, half-listening, or dreaming, in escape from the tasks they did not comprehend or had not the vitality to tackle. Like dance and drama, music reaches the child very directly and intimately. His body makes the sound; he sings, plucks, hits, or blows.

Children need a rich diet of music. One can never be certain how children of any ability or age will receive music and one must be prepared to offer great variety, jazz and "pop", music which has stood the test of time, modern music of all kinds, and sounds from instruments of many kinds. All must be of a high standard according to its kind. We need to have good sound for children, particularly for these children. There is no time or effort to waste on poor music, or on poor reproduction, no risk can be taken when so much has to be accomplished. These children will not grow in understanding or personality if offered only babyish material. We must not make the mistake in music which has been made in supplying reading material for these pupils.

These children may not be going to become musicians, but music is not their failure, and we can use this pathway as one which they can tread reasonably normally as they develop and gain help in the ways in which they do fail. Music can help the growth of word language which is vital. They can have experiences of sounds about which they can talk. Music is fast, happy, slow, calm, loud, strong. What does it sound like to you? This music has sounds of the sea, this has the buzzing of the bee, this has a lovely tune, high up, thin and clear, and this has a strong beat, it makes you move your hands and feet. The imagination may play freely and here dramatic music is important. Just as important, however, is the need to direct children's attention to the music itself, to the quality of the sounds, the shape of the melody, the stresses and phrases, the climaxes and decrescendos, using words which the children can understand, and encouraging them to use words which they find descriptive and appropriate. Singing songs can be a very helpful approach to the use of words, their sounds, and their meanings. Singing can bring freedom of flow and ease to the child who has marked stammer or defect in speech continuity. Speech defects are so common among these children and singing is so beneficial in this way, that for this reason alone it would merit an important place in the school programme.

Music can be a part of everyday pleasure, to celebrate a birthday, to welcome the day or the season, to enrich life at any time. Always there will be room to sing, even if dance is not possible. The class teacher can relate music to other activities; only he can really make music a part of the day's programme. He may not be a fine musician, but he must like music, believe in its value, and explore bravely. There is room for the specialist and for the visitor who can bring fine, live music to the children; there is a place for the radio, the record player, tape recorder, and television, and, of course, for the visit to the concert hall.

Children of all abilities can make music in many ways. Some instruments they can make or help to make. These include shakers, wooden blocks, and simple drums, even simple stringed instruments. Percussion instruments, simple melodic instruments, strings to pluck or hit, xylophones, and glockenspiels, melodicas, recorders, and guitars, are all possible for some children in these groups. One must try all available musical possibilities and be ready for surprises when one finds unexpected ability and ready to use ingenuity to ensure that a child does not face severe failure with any instrument. Playing an instrument, however simple, means a great deal to a child; it really belongs to him, becoming an extension of himself. Repetition is advantageous and familiarity brings success and progress. Radio and television theme tunes and a repertoire of songs and tunes are good. There must be acquaintance with music from an early stage.

Where, then, are the chief difficulties for some of these children? Many cannot concentrate for very long, and therefore songs and music must be short and the teacher must be observant and sensitive to this factor. Sometimes a teacher will find that the children cannot absorb sound as quickly as most, and that the very quick tempo is best avoided. It is important, however, not to lose quality of liveliness in music, but to choose the music carefully, avoiding that which flows very rapidly. Sometimes children are timid in being alone in the sound they make. This is so with all classes in all schools and groups, but for these children such insecurity could be severely detracting from confidence and growth and is best avoided. Mr. Dobbs blames a weak memory for the lack of progress made in some of these groups. Some tire very quickly when working intensely and short periods of effort are preferable to attempts to master a tune in a single lesson. Some of the children have difficulties brought about by catarrh or by frequent colds, some have poor postural characteristics so that breathing is not as full or easy as with the normal child. Music notation can be for them extremely difficult and may be yet another task in which they are destined to find no interest or joy or success.

Yet these children so often show such perseverance, they retain music once it has been learned so well and have such obvious joy in their success.

A.S.M.—G*

> When movement is allied to music it is generally true to say that the better the quality of the movement produced the more valuable and concentrated will have been the listening and the richer the musical experience.*

We have already discussed from the movement point of view the relationship between music and movement. Music is linked closely with movement and dance and movement is especially for many of these children a very direct and intimate way in which sound, rhythm, phrasing, melody, and musical shape and form can be experienced. Kinaesthetic and musical awareness will happen at times and degrees individual to each child, but a teacher can be very aware of these opportunities for musical education, when expression and reaction through movement will readily take place. As meaningful experiences arise in the integration of ideas and stimuli, the qualities of sound are allied with those of movement. The body responds readily to pulse and rhythm. Rhythmic memory is usually more developed at all stages of childhood than tonal memory, and both more keenly than pitch. The making of sounds through beating and clapping, playing instruments, or singing are extensions of bodily movement. When moving to music, children may listen through active participation, being in this way assisted in the process of listening. They can lose themselves while dancing to music, in a world of movement and sound. For these children this, for a small part of the school day, is a good experience, relieving tension, and bringing to them freer flow of bodily movement. Children can dance with their drum or shaker, making music as they go. They can also accompany or stimulate another's dance.

This alliance of dance and music comes easily about when the mood or story of the music stimulates dance drama. Music which expresses the mood and quality of morning, of the midnight witchery, or of winter, or music which tells a story, becomes familiar to children as they are partners with it in dance.

The nature of musical ability is a complicated thing. There is a great range of ability. One does find among children who have not succeeded in the skills of reading, writing, and number

* J. Dobbs, *loc. cit.*

some who have marked music ability. Where this is so, great steps forward can be taken in the development of the child, if such ability can be recognized and fostered. For all children, however, there should be the lifelong enjoyment of music. Here exists a possible interest and love for an adult who is likely to have to live by means of a routine, monotonous job. Most important at this time there is here another language whereby these children may communicate. Our task is to investigate fully the possibilities of music making for all children, to persuade teachers that music is not only the prerogative of the musician, and that all sensitive teachers who love music can help children to explore sound, to make music, and to enjoy it. Musical education is making progress. The followers of Carl Orff and educators who have related ideas are doing much to expand the world of music for all children. It is important that this work should take place fully in special schools and departments because the need of these children for communication of this kind is great.

Other Activities which play an Important Part in Communication

Everything that proceeds from where the child is in skill and understanding can contribute educationally for the children who do not readily succeed in school. There are schools and classes for less able children where they work freely and actively, experiencing and exploring their environment, and learning by doing, one interest leading to another. Very often an extremely good teacher leads the children through good relationship, care, and vitality, to interests which contribute to their understanding of language and number, as well as to their own personal growth, and educates them widely in the matters of the world.

All these are valuable and are not pushed aside as second rate in favour of more purely expressive activities. Accent is placed on the arts because they offer a nearness to the emotional life of the child, and the need for emotional growth is great for these particular children. Integration, fashionable as that word has become in education, often means that one uses the arts to bring to expression and to consolidation experiences involving history, geography, biology, and mathematics. Integration of the arts themselves is so often interpreted as a production, involving the making of scenery and costumes, music, drama, and the dance. These are of great and obvious value for many reasons, but the arts are themselves vehicles of communication. They need occasions of non-predestination, so that a child is really free to use art for his own needs and to serve it in his own way. They touch and educate deeply if allowed to do so, and integrated projects will be better served by the concentration and discipline of each area of expression for some part of the time.

Art engages the whole person, physical, sensory, intellectual, emotional, and spiritual. The arts are concerned with the worthwhileness of living, with vision, with wonder, with the opening of new dimensions, with the setting aside of fixed ideas.

There are some other activities which contribute decidedly to personality growth and to communication for children, if they are approached sympathetically and sincerely from the children's point of view. These include physical education, religious education, the keeping of a garden, and the care of animals. It would seem to be desirable to include some brief discussion of these because of the special contribution which they can make.

Physical Education

In its most educational aspects physical education does include exploring and creating with movement language, and this part of physical education most certainly does offer children a chance to communicate ideas. In this way I would include physical education as I would include the preparatory stages of the language of dance.

What then of other aspects? There are the gymnastic skills, games, athletics, swimming, and outdoor pursuits of all kinds. How much can participation in these activities contribute to the communicating child?

Dr. Oliver has shown us the tremendous effect of physical activity, well sponsored and led, and well provided for in material, on the wellbeing, attitudes and abilities in this and other spheres of activity, for the less able child.*

One cannot generalize about the ability to acquire physical skill or about the benefits to be gained from physical activity, too much, where these children are concerned. There are among them those who are physically less healthy, less robust than most children, some have minor physical handicaps, many have not quick reaction, and many have unusually limited physical awareness and control. A large number have a poor background of social awareness and make relationships only with difficulty, so that when sharing apparatus or playing team games they are likely to be fussy and unco-operative. Many come from deprived homes. They may be poorly clad and less clean than ordinary children and so are uncomfortable when showering and changing. The homes from which these children may well come often encourage children to be bodily fussy and the child complains of trivial ailments. These groups do, of course, include children who suffer more than most from colds and headaches, and who tend to be accident prone. There are also, as we have seen, children who are under sedation, those who are liable to epileptic fits, or who have an abnormal heart condition. Obviously these children must receive special care from teachers who know them well, are observant, and sympathetic in an intelligent, human manner. Moreover, they are often unreliable; they forget their equipment, having less often the backing of a co-operative home.

So we find that sometimes the specialist teacher of physical education, like some specialist housecraft teachers and musicians, has no great liking for these classes when they are in a secondary school with games, matches and other competitions looming large upon the programme. They cannot be of much use in teams because they tend to be unreliable, they cannot stay to practices,

* J. N. Oliver, The interchange between the various growth characteristics of educationally subnormal boys in residential schools, Ph.D. thesis, University of Birmingham, 1962–63.

and mother keeps them at home on Saturday mornings. It must, however, be said that there are teachers of physical education who, because of the nature of their interest in child development and because many are educated well in their colleges, contribute very well indeed to the education of the special classes. If one considers the contribution which physical education could make to the personality growth of these children, however, one must be aware of the difficulties for them in competition with groups of less handicapped children, and the danger of further failure where they are concerned.

On the other hand, there are many physical activities which are not immediately competitive, through which these children could receive much help—bodily, mentally, and emotionally. They need so badly the stimulation, enjoyment, and increase in bodily awareness, which good physical education can bring. They need the specialist care which Dr. Oliver gave to the boys he taught— good apparatus, the interest of the specialist teachers and advisers behind the work, and, of course, the familiar, caring teacher whom they trust implicitly. They need a special share of the swimming and athletic facilities. Conditions need to be generous for them, they need more time, more coaching, more material, so that they have their share of success. They need success in attainment more than the children in the more academically successful groupings. Here they stand some chance of succeeding.

Where facilities are concerned children in the special classes in the ordinary school suffer more than those who attend a special school. The special school is small and apparatus can be more easily shared than in the large school where the remedial stream receives so often a poor portion. Where teams are concerned they are not in competition with their more skilful, stronger fellows. On the other hand, if a school which is large and well equipped, does have a sympathetic and understanding head and specialist staff, possibilities can be very favourable for these children.

Outdoor activities are especially good. The possibilities of walking, climbing, camping, and exploring, for many of these children are immense, and the total educative value of such activities is emphatic. They involve the direct experience of learning about historical and geographical things, about people and the man-made world, and natural life, the gaining of social awareness, and the making of relationships. They will see and be among lively and interesting things; the senses will be awakened and the whole body stimulated in the open air.

Swimming, too, offers particular value if taught sympathetically. There is a tremendous thrill for any child who reaches the day when he can swim across the bath. Once confidence is gained, most of the children in special education, whom we discuss, even those with poor balance or a physical handicap, can learn to swim. Some are very timid and withdrawn, and although for them the approach must be intensely sympathetic, success in swimming may be a major step in development, as well as giving safeguard against accident.

Physical education then can contribute enormously to the situation whereby a person may be helped to a state of mind and body conducive to interest and learning. Children may become more awake, more lively, and released from excessive body tension. Success may be attained even in a small skill mastered or improved upon. Through activity with balls, bats, and other games apparatus, many children can work out their aggressive feelings which might otherwise find less favourable outlets. One has only to watch a boy throwing a ball with all his might against a wall to observe the outpouring of emotional and physical energy which initiates the loud plop of the ball against the wall and the force of its return. Destructiveness and frustration can often be released if the teacher can see the need and provide the opportunity for activities which do this harmlessly and positively.

There is the utmost need for the care of the body where such children are concerned. Somehow one must help the body to co-operate in the quest for energy, self-respect, and confidence. It is true that much of the drooping attitude and dull-eyed slackness of tone which characterises the posture of less able children results from depression of mind and spirit, but the body is an important factor. Some of these children need physiotherapy to help their bodies when they are suffering from a handicap which distorts their balance and posture, or their ability to use the body normally, and there is urgent necessity for more physio-therapy for such children. These, however, and all others need to enjoy physical activity, to be helped to use the body sensitively and well, by a teacher who really understands human movement quality.

Physical education can help children to value cleanliness and good standards of behaviour towards one another. It can help them to have healthy attitudes about the care of the body, and in the hands of caring, intelligent teachers can really assist the growing up processes which are sometimes so difficult for them.

So long as physical education activities do not put these children in a situation of failure, they may help very much to make them more ready for communication and for learning.

The Garden

Often one finds children in special schools and in special classes taking a great interest in the garden. Many special schools are surrounded by extensive grounds, and though these are often formally laid and well tended, there is sometimes ground which the children have as their own. In a country which is to a growing extent, as people acquire their small gardens, a nation of garden makers, this interest in growing plants and planning gardens is valuable and may be a lasting asset. We have often teachers who are genuinely interested in gardening and so we find in many schools that this is a major concern. Indeed, in one school where as an outsider, I thought that the love, devotion, and educational enthusiasm of the teacher–gardener must be for the intense good of the children, I found that some of the older children were "really fed up with gardening". It would seem that the teacher's enthusiasm had gone ahead of her understanding of the more easily bored children. However, there is no doubt that the activity is a good one, through which children can learn directly about the nature of living things, can have joy and interest, can perhaps develop patience, can certainly have healthful and productive activity in the open air and start a love which may continue throughout their lives.

With a wise teacher who is prepared to submerge his own preferences and guide tactfully, they can help to plan and to create, to develop the caring attitude which grows side by side with love, and can derive much satisfaction. This love contributes to the enjoyment of beautiful things, to the world of design, decoration, shape, and form, in which we hope they will take part.

One finds in schools sometimes that the children not only garden because of the wonder and joy of growing things, but because there has developed a commercial interest. The urge to make money is very strong and the incentive to grow in order to sell is great. Here, however, is the origin of much experience, not only of plants, soils, and fertilisers, but of prices, numbers, gain, and loss. There is also the satisfaction on the part of the children and teachers of using money which they have really earned, for an extra visit, some new gramophone records, or piece of equipment which they would like to possess as a group. Such mercenary activity must of course be limited. My chief delight in it is that the children will thereby pursue through necessity the arts of counting, measuring, and dealing precisely with number and materials.

Most important is the fact that for them the garden is of itself a place of purposeful enjoyment, where one does not compete with one's fellows but where one competes and co-operates with nature only, and whereby one may help the creative process and become part of it.

Keeping Animals

In schools for educationally subnormal children, particularly in residential schools, one often finds that as in a good Infant School, children have fish, rabbits, guinea-pigs, doves, and even a donkey, goat, or pony in their care. Often there is a cat or dog belonging to the Head or to a member of staff, but being very much a member of the community.

Those children need very much to give love and care, and keeping pets helps the residential children to participate in an activity which is part of everyday normal living. They need to be able to lavish affection and to give effort in caring for animals much more than the child in a normal happy home. Often these children's first real and confident relationships are made with animals. They talk to them with expression, without inhibition, with naturalness, and love.

Through their care for animals they learn practically which is for them a very important way of learning. They can use their practical skills in the construction of cages, huts, and runs, they can learn about food values and cleanliness, and they can learn about the nature of life and its reproduction. This is an avenue of practical learning which invites full participation, but is also a way whereby the children can lavish care and find themselves essentially needed.

Religious Education

This is a very difficult subject to teach, even when a teacher has belief in its place in education and greatly desires to make this contribution. When one is thinking of children for whom the language of words is impoverished, there is very great difficulty in interpretation of religious concepts. It is important to discuss religious education here, because there can be a communicating aspect which, given the right situation and personnel, would be extremely important, but in less good circumstances there is danger of confusion and worry for the children through lack of understanding. There were the children who were being "taught" the story of the crossing of the Red Sea. They were restless and the story was interrupted constantly by admonitions. Afterwards the child with whom I had been sitting, asked with a puckered face, "What's a Miracle?" On the other hand, I visited one school in particular where the whole atmosphere seemed to radiate from the personality of the Head, a sincerely religious man, who carried from the morning assembly, through the day, his faith and the spirit of worship.

What then of religious education for these children? How can we give them awareness of the meaningful and significant things of life and influence their attitudes and relationships, strengthening them against adversity? True religion must be conveyed by people, by their way of life, responses to everyday difficulties and opportunities. In this way one communicates to children honesty and love. These qualities must be seen and known to invade the whole of school life. The less able child deserves a special measure of kindness, tolerance, and generosity. For many there is great confusion between home and school. They must learn to give sympathy and love, yet at home maybe, to receive little. They must learn that honesty is right whilst they live amongst dishonesty and are impressed with the importance of material gain. In the street and even in school they are likely to receive unkindnesses. It is therefore of the utmost importance that teachers communicate to these children attitudes of such a nature, that they stand clearly and impress deeply. Every topic and every action enters into this teaching.

Often the daily assembly and the whole aspect of worship plays a large part in the school day. Children enjoy the sense of order, pattern and peace; they enjoy to sing, listen, and use words which are lovely, to attend to something apart from learning, without struggling, which may be little understood, yet which enriches the day, giving trust, and safety. One would not wish this experience to be lost for the children but that it should be full of sincerity and beauty and that it should be a total experience, unhindered by notice rendering or admonishment. I recall a school in Minneapolis, U.S.A., The Sheltering Arms School, where the children were extremely handicapped mentally and some physically. These children had a service in the chapel every week. The choir was dressed, the ritual was complete, and even though there was, I believe, very little understanding, the ordered ritual gave inner quiet and deep satisfaction to many of these restless and often disturbed children. The Festivals of the Church can be for these young people particularly special times. Children need meaningful occasions in their lives, times when there is colour, music, ritual, and an atmosphere which is different from everyday. Making school life rich in this way, uplifts and energizes, and helps in the understanding of worship.

Without doubt one must include in this part of education discussion of life's problems. This is more important in some aspects for the children in question than for any others. It must take place at the level of the children's own thoughts and abilities of course, there must be talk about everyday things of life, they must be free to ask, to tell, and to express their fears and lack of understanding.

It is relevant to speak here of the need for some teachers to have a special relationship with children so that each child may feel that there is in school or in her church someone to whom she might talk individually, that there is a mother or father figure available.

Finally, these children are great helpers. They serve eagerly if allowed to do so, and can make their contribution to a community as well as other children, even especially well. This can be a starting point of expressing Christian attitudes and of gaining joy for them in useful activity.

CHAPTER 13

THE WRITTEN LANGUAGE

IN OLDER societies the ability to use the written word denoted a social role. It belonged to religion and the State and so to the scholar. Later it was necessary also for the merchant, but only in our time have reading and writing become accepted as the birth-right of all and as a necessary part of life. Even though there are communities where the written word would appear still to be hardly a necessity, we tend to regard with horror the figures which attempt to estimate illiteracy in the world. In 1837 over one-half of the children in England, in 1872 one third of France, and in 1950 two out of five in the world were illiterate. Neverthe-less, progress at least in Europe has been rapid. In 1966 only less than 3 per cent of French people were illiterate and here in Britain there is great outcry when research projects emerge with conflicting reports of the inability of junior children to read and write.

Speech is the bond which establishes society. Man alone has acquired the ability to communicate through speech. We must give verbal language pride of place when we consider communi-cation. This is the medium which the children who concern us in this study will use, to assent, to state facts, to give information, to express desires and ideas, and to communicate their thought. They will include silent speech and thinking aloud, words and actions being bound up together. The sounds of words give pleasure and excitement. Words must be spoken to reach their full expressiveness. So children must talk. Reading is dependent upon the spoken language, writing upon the integration of reading and speaking.

Adult reading needs may be relatively few, but those few are important. Literacy is important; it is modern, it is, of course, artificial and only possible if one knows the code. Children growing up in this society must, if possible, be able to use our code fluently in order that their lives may be efficient and that education may be fully open to them. Most important, they must become literate to nourish their own self-image and to acquire a recognized place in the community for which to a great extent literacy means respectability in that illiteracy does not.

> A man set out from Buxton for an interview for a job in Camberwell and was found six hours later, wandering around the Elephant and Castle, as he hadn't dared to ask anyone to read him the names on the front of the buses.

> Evening classes for adult illiterates have been tried in many areas and have failed because people do not like their illiteracy brought to the notice of the others in the class. A middle aged man refused to have lessons from a woman because he could not bear the ignominy of revealing his inabilities to his sexual inferior.*

Jonathan Miller in a recent lecture spoke of the snobbery of the book and the way in which the written word signifies for people "truth" as against any other kind of information given by film, theatre, television, or the spoken word. "The book," he said, "is sacred and slow."† True as this is, and much as one ponders over the prized position of the written and printed word, it would be risking too much for children to ignore the urgent necessity for them to master this language. Books are the sources of material from which we can choose; they store it for re-reading at one's own rate and in one's own time. Man's knowledge has continuity in this way and the accumulation of knowledge is stored and much effort and time saved in consequence.

Language is a living thing, flexible and adaptable as new needs for words and phrases arise, yet it is stable enough to make understanding of near generations secure. Indeed, our spelling has become almost frozen, leading to the difficulties which children and adults encounter in mastering the symbols.

* A. Hurst, Help for illiterates, *New Society*, September 1966.
† Lecture by Jonathan Miller, Leicester Art Gallery, 4 April 1962.

Language influences the whole of the psychological life of man. Where there are words to express he understands, and the richness of his understanding goes alongside the richness of the language. "Words are the life blood of culture."*

In education we cannot depart from words. The more specialized and complex the subject, the more complex is the language. With the written language we can abolish the barriers of distance and time; we are heirs of history and of the increasing legacies of books. Words are, of course, open to misunderstanding and, as well as offering mutual sharing of ideas, they provide division between men who have their differing languages. Books are still the main tool of the teacher in spite of increasing accent in school upon doing creative work with other media, and upon teaching machines, television, broadcast, and computers. People, however, are tending more and more to be reduced to spectator level, communication becoming one way, and many people find little inclination or necessity to read for themselves.

Yet still this legacy must be replanted. If we are to think of these special children as persons who are important in the community, their teaching to be regarded with the greatest optimism, we must consider it essential that they leave school able to handle the written and printed language, remembering that words are but instruments and mean nothing by themselves.

We think perhaps first of the need for such a child to master language for the practical necessities of his life, but we must go on to consider the implications of language mastery, his ability to think, and to grow in understanding. "Language then, encompasses the ability to abstract, to attach meaning to words, and to employ words as symbols for thought, and for the expression of ideas."†

Let us look for a moment at the variety of symbols which children may be required to master in school: words, perhaps I.T.A. and the transference to the accepted spelling, numbers and symbols of measurement, musical signs, and for children in

* P. Meredith, *Instruments of Communication*, p. 8.
† H. R. Myklebust, *Development and Disorder of Written Language*, p. 2.

"normal" classes possibly a foreign language, scientific and mathematical symbols of a more advanced nature, and the possible addition of kinetography or movement writing.

Children can master skills well, and the acquisition of symbols may present little problem to the successfully learning child if he has understanding of the process. It is essential, then, that the skill of using the written language, so elusive so often for the less able child, is related to the meaningful art of speaking and to those other more available languages of drawing, painting, moving, dancing, and acting, and to the active, doing life which brings him into contact with the world around. Reading and writing, probably foremost in the minds of teachers of special schools and classes for less able children, has been left to the end. It is important that these skills shall be means of communication, not stumbling, isolated words, or mechanical reading, but language that they shall comprehend not only with the eye but with the mind. It is vital that there is not developed a hostility to reading, that a child attempts to express, and that his efforts receive acceptance and assistance. Teachers become skilled at seeing through the queer attempts at word formation and correlation and can, with their experience, come to understand some of a child's common difficulties and so help.

Problems encountered with reading and writing have so often been the beginning of many other difficulties, offering a major contribution to failure in school and leading to embarrassment, humiliation, frustration, and rapidly to the state of affairs where general non-learning sets in. It is reasonably easy in a large class of infant children, taught by an inexperienced and perhaps harassed teacher, in a school where activity abounds, for the avoidance of reading to be overlooked. It is even more likely to happen that a child finds success in reading difficult where activity is not stimulating to the desire to seek words. The child arriving as a non-reader in the junior school can already be looked upon as backward, and so the train of events can become established. The child is a non-reader, losing faith in himself and regarding reading as the focus of his difficulties.

Reading problems can have many and varied causes, neurological, and psychological, but the largest number originate in educational defects, whatever else may have contributed, and it is with these that this book is concerned. If the difficulties which block the ability for these children to read can be overcome, the outlook and learning prospect for them will be much more healthy. As they master the language of the written word we must make sure that interest is maintained, that reading matter is stimulating, whilst remaining within and or near to the level of skill acquired. There is a tremendous need for books which, whilst simple in word usage and sentence construction, contain interesting material for a child whether he is 9 or 15 years of age. What senior child would wish to work at his reading if that which he unveils tells him the story of children playing in the garden or going on a picnic. This problem is recognized and attempts are being made to remedy the situation, but so often by teachers who do not really know the children concerned well enough, even though they believe that they do, or by those not working closely enough with the children, by a man teacher who does not consider the girls, or vice versa.

These children have a poverty of vocabulary. Words they know tend quite naturally to be those which are important in their lives; Friday, Saturday, and Sunday were more familiar words for a group of children than the names of the other days in the week; foods and drinks are named more readily, and one teacher found that her pupils labelled extremely backward, retained and named long lists of pop singers and songs. The implications are obvious, and these give us a starting point.

Speech defects, so common among these children, hinder their grasp of words, as when a child persisted in attempts to write "paper cheeses" in a story, meaning "baby Jesus", although here one would wonder if the teacher had had a bad cold. Such speech difficulties have detracted already from the motivation to communicate and have probably contributed to personality problems and insecurity.

Writing and reading, like speaking, need a recipient. Just as the child must listen, there must be for him a listener. They have often a very short memory span and need constant help, much patience, and encouragement. There is in fact a need for remarkable teachers. But we have some remarkable teachers and many potential teachers who will be remarkable. There is the reward of intense joy for a child at the slightest achievement, yet the danger of setback with the natural desire on the part of a teacher to over-press and accelerate progress. The ever-present reading age may be a guide to a teacher, but presents a risk. A child has individual personal difficulties which are not easily related to those of anyone else. Children need different approaches, different aspects of encouragement and praise, urging and challenging. They need time in their own stages, time to consolidate, and to be ready to go on.

As we have seen, the family is so often a source of deprivation, both in the poverty of the spoken word and in the fact of non-literacy, and lack of incentive to read and write for a child. "I am the only one, but still I am the one. I cannot do everything. But still I can do something. And because I cannot do everything I will not refuse to do something I can do."*

The stress must be on expressing. All experience helps, and none is wasted. They need to be with words, to see words, to write, and to go on writing. Words must become necessary.

One cannot force them forward, but as things are worth expressing, as someone wants them expressed, with the confidence given by expressing in all fields of activity, they may enlarge the range of these particular skills. One must speak to them especially in terms of relationships and sequences of time as they find these concepts difficult; difficulties will require a teacher's skill, but all the time there must be expanding interest and experience developing through the world they are in. We learn to use language by practising it as a manifestation of the whole being with awareness of communication.

* E. E. Hale, quoted from Dr. Maria Egg-Benes, *World Health Organization, Forward Trends*, Summer–Autumn, 1962.

Furthermore, there is in my mind no doubt that the readiness of children to write and the quality of their writing is influenced by opportunities to express their thoughts through materials such as paint, clay, and dramatic movement.*

There is such great anxiety in our community about reading and writing. It is certainly important and I would not wish to minimize the seriousness of the child entering even the junior school without the developing ability to use the written word. The printed word possesses enormous wealth, and in the realm of writing at any level is the opportunity for expression. So, alongside the urge in school for "creative writing" is the tremendous pressure upon children, and indeed upon anxious teachers and parents, to succeed in implanting the mastery of the written word. We have I.T.A., teaching machines, television, numerous games, charts, and graded books, and endless reading schemes. Some of these are very good in that they spark off understanding for some children. Where there is difficulty, where the rich environment and care of the usual good infant school does not succeed in bringing about progress in mastery, then some special way might help, as it certainly does with immigrant children who have a special problem. Indeed, the children we are discussing have special problems.

It is, however, with the nature of life for these children that this work is concerned. Reading and writing will only become worth while and meaningful; it is likely that they will only last, if they arise alongside interest, happiness in success, and the knowledge that the secrets of the written word are worth unfolding. "The value of the educational experience should be assessed in terms of its total impact on the pupils, skills, qualities and personal development, not by basic attainment alone."†

Wherever one visits a class for the slower learners, a remedial group or a special school, quite naturally, and perhaps at this time, rightly, a tremendous accent is placed upon reading and writing. Teachers recognize the results of early failure to read and

* A. B. Clegg (Ed.), *The Excitement of Writing*, p. 28.
† *Half our Future*, Newsom Committee, H.M.S.O., p. 31.

A.S.M.—H

write, and they take what appear to be the most direct ways to remedy the situation. Even with the crudity of approach that often operates, there is success, there is progress; more children are learning to read in our slow-learning classes and schools. There is tremendous variation. One comes across reading and writing ability which is near "normal" in a residential special school and almost total inability in another, and severe illiteracy among seniors in the "bottom stream" of a secondary school.

It is difficult to ascertain the ability of pupils because teachers are often very unwilling to allow one to have the children's unaided writing, but when one is successful in getting this it compares, most often, very badly with that which might have been helped a great deal by the teacher. Nevertheless, there is great variation and no doubt at all that where the climate of the school is progressive and where the children are expressing deeply, there is some very exciting and often fluent writing. The most meaningful and communicative writing I found was in two schools, both of which put great accent on painting, movement, dance and drama, and upon the whole of the expressive side of education. This may have been accidental and aided by my own wishful thinking, but it nevertheless was so.

Many schools had their own reading schemes. Some I could not comprehend fully, but many deal with words only, e.g. words of type IT, words of types POI, OD $\triangledown$, DAT.

Most schools were very honest—even cynical—about the children's difficulties, and teachers talked of the inability of the children to recall the correct words when they needed them, the problem for them of abstract words and of compound sentences. They complained about the quality of the language, the innumerable "and's" and "there's" and the repetitive nature of statements.

Yet when the children really experienced, when their feelings were alerted, and most of all when they succeeded, expressiveness began to grow. It is certain that the drilling of words, of sentence making, and of word recognition by repetition will be of limited use unless it goes hand in hand with awakening, pleasure, excitement, and with understanding.

In order not constantly to interrupt the script, there follows a collection of children's writing which illustrates to some extent the heights and depths of their ability.*

* See Appendix.

CONCLUSION

Darwin held the opinion, as a result of a life-time of observation, that men differ less in capacity than in zeal and determination to use the powers they have.*

Among the children called educationally subnormal, or backward, or slow learners, or less able, there are children who for various reasons have less capacity for learning as we present it in school, than others, but for many the misfortunes of their early lives or the accidents of their educative experience have brought about an incompatibility which has led to learning difficulties.

It is in the realm of the emotional life that our children are least served in education. Often we must give children a chance to grow up again as they should have done, to be loved with unashamedness, to enjoy simple things which should have been surrounded by love much earlier, eating, talking, being close together, and being accorded the dignity of having an eager listener who cares, in a situation where the individual is all important.

The problem is great and is complicated and increased by the accent in education upon acquisition of knowledge and the attainment of qualification. The problem for the slowest learners tends ironically to be increased as the educational opportunity becomes more equally shared.

Many people work extremely hard for the less able child. Is it possible that we should be ready to think again and try avenues of activities which, entered into fully, may mean delaying still further the apparent acquisition of reading and writing skills, but which ultimately might well help these children to become individuals who can take a confident place in this harsh world of rush and competition, who have come to terms with ultimate

* E. Conklin, *Heredity and Environment*, p. 314.

values and who might in many cases master the use of the written word because it has come to have meaning.

Through participating in the visual arts, movement, dance, drama, and music, a person comes to relationship with and understanding of the world around and the verbal language which it uses as he can in no other way. Many people believe this.

I cannot measure this work or prove that these ways will succeed. There is much evidence that they will in those schools where the arts are being used as educative forces and, indeed, in the communicating personalities of children and students who have had opportunities to work expressively and have found freedom and success.

How is it to be done? Where are the teachers to teach in this way? It may well be that only when we have really educated children fully, and by fully I mean as freely-thinking, expressive, confident people, shall we be able to call upon those who can teach with understanding the children who fail to "learn". There are, however, many avenues and many teachers will follow one or two or more. Interlacing drives provide incentives for learning. Many teachers of the less able child are trying to teach unwilling and unmotivated people. The self-satisfied are poor learners and the depressed and failing are too.

We cannot afford to waste time and we cannot afford to waste people. It is urgent that we look at the failure in our educational world and remedy it because we have, if we do not, an increasing problem as schools become larger, educational methods less personal, and the world a less "cosy" place.

One must find stimuli, understand failure, initiate success, and reward it with pleasure and praise. There will be dignity, adventure and gaiety. "'Learning' is something that you do for yourself and for others with others."*

* Professor J. Tibble, at the conference discussing future work for the Handicapped Child, Wye College, Kent, 19–21 April 1963.

CHILDREN'S WRITING

IN ORDER to avoid constantly interrupting the discussion, I have included examples of children's writing which illustrate some of the points made as an appendix.

These children, as if aware of their limited ability to use words, very often choose to illustrate their writing with drawings and paintings which are usually far more expressive than the words. They enjoy to decorate the pages as if to compensate for their poverty.

There is tremendous variation in writing ability from school to school, the work in special schools sometimes being more accomplished than that in remedial classes and the lowest streams in the ordinary schools. It is extremely difficult to obtain untouched writing and one can only guess to what extent the spelling and sentence construction are a child's own. Teachers wish only to be helpful and most often, in their loyalty, do not readily give away very limited work.

The factors illustrated by the writing included are the starkness of the statements made and their repetition, the way in which those things which are very important to a child emerge, even when expression for other things is not available, and the liveliness and fluency of some of the writing from schools where expressive activities are very much fostered.

The residential special school from which I borrowed the following pieces of work was, of all the schools which I visited, one of those which appeared to the observer and visiting teacher rich in expressive activity which contributed to the learning situation.

The school had within it children with major learning problems and some whose greatest difficulty was their maladjustment.

All children had problems which affected their learning in school.

Girl Aged 15 years.

BEAUTIFUL THINGS

There lived a little girl, Her name was Susson, Her Mother and Farther promised her when Susson growes up, That She will have alot of monny, And that time came, Susson had a lot of monny, And When She went to work She urnd a good deal of monny, Untill Susson Was very rich, She loved pretty things, So Susson got a beautiful Cottage, A fine dress for her self With loverly black Velvet and Some Seaquins, And She bought some gorgors jewels. They glittered like Crown jewels, Susson had gorgors dimonds, Saphires roobbys and emerals and moon stones, And lotes of uther stones, And Susson had a gorgors lot of rings and ear rings and brooches and things like that. And She got a lot of lovely things for her house, She had a lot of artifishal flowers. And Susson had a lovely gold moste gorgors Wole paper, That you could think off, It had silver leaves and red roses, and her home Was so gorgors that it nearly looked like a pretty palace but small, It had a big shanderlir in the dinning hall, And a big glass table looking very posh, And gold certons With silver pattons on, Susson had a lovely lot of dresses, Every body loved her home, And Susson Was a very kind person, She gave some of her monny to all the poor people, And to the OXFam even more monny than enny body els, Well Susson had every think she could wish for and she was Very happy, Susson had a gorgors gardon, With Two lips and rosses croceses and honeysuckles, And a big bridge of rosses going across. When the King knew about it, He told her if she would like to marry the prince, and Susson said yes, And they both marryed happyly ever after.

Girl Aged 14 years.
This girl has a very great interest in animals.

REVEL HEAD

I know a little pony
his name is Revel Head
I took him to the vet
To see about his leg
and do you know what
the vet said
"He told poor Revel to go to bed."

There are pictures of ponies, frogs, birds, and dogs, the latter named Gilly and Buddy-Biddy. There are drawings of the things one needs for riding—hat, gloves, breeches, and jacket, boots and whip all labelled carefully. The things you need for the horse are also drawn and labelled with great detail—the saddle, brush, "reigns" and shoes.

Girl Aged 14 years.

This girl writes about keeping a puppy, training dogs, getting a dog ready for a show, then about more horses' needs. Covering twenty sides of a notebook she writes "Smoky the Story of a Foal", then "The Dog's Diary", and "The Horses Diary". Her examination essay was called "Puppy for Sale".

PUPPY FOR SALE

Once upon a time. There was a lady selling puppies. She was saying puppies for sale. When up came a little girl. The lady said. "What is your name." She said. "my name is Sally." "O thats a very nice name you have." Whitch puppy would you like. This one said Sally. Sally said thank-you and she ran of home. Sally told her mum. Sally said is it alright if I have the puppy. Yes my dear you may have him. "His name is going to be Cimber." Cimber was all black except in the chest. It was all white. I do love you Cimber said Sally. I will never let you go. Sally took the dog out for a walk. They went over three Meadows. Cimber was very delighted when he was in the meadows. He saw a lots of rabbits. He saw one rabbit hopping a different way from all the others. Cimber thought he would follow it. so he did. When he got there. He couldnt find no rabbit at all. He couldnt find his way out. Every where he looked there was nothing but trees. Sally ran over to where he was and picked him up. "Come on your coming home with me." When they got home. He had some Pal meat. "Cor Cimber youve had a real long walk." Now you can go to bed.

Senior Girl.

BEAUTIFUL THINGS

God made things. Why did he make Beautiful things, for us to look at, for instns birds and trees, He made the birs to fly and sing songs. But can we sing like birds no he made us all different too, and he made the fish, he made everything, and flowers to grow, and he made everything interestsing too like shells are good to look at and the shapes are interesting as well, He made the butterflies, and they Beautiful things all colours, and he made name for all the Animals, names like Bubger, And he made dog for the blind, and you have Animals for petstoo, God made everything in is word, and he made man and man discoverd things in this world too, And God made us to love the enermy as a friend, And God made the fields.

This special day school was another where the environment was rich and much use was made of the visual arts, movement, dance, and drama. I was not surprised to find that here there was a great deal of very lively writing accompanied by extremely expressive drawing. These children had many experiences.

All the writers were between 10 and 16 years. In some cases only, an indication of the level of ability was given to me in the form of an I.Q. measurement.

This writing was accompanied by a very lively picture of the glassworks.

One day we went to Knottingley. We went on a single decker bus and the glassworks was called Jacksons. We went on Wednesday When we got there we went in and we went in a lot of rooms and there was about 2 or 3 We went and they were very hot. because they had a furnace in. And they make glass out of sand and limestone. Then we saw a lot of jam jars and they were all sizes.

DAVE CLARKE FIVE

I think Dave Clarke Five has a good beat and a good song
I hope next week they will be at number one in the hit parade and Cilla Black gets knocked out.

On Saturday CaG Rugby team won the fird round of the Yorsher cup I hope they will get the cup this year

Thre boys were in the house. The boys got behind a cupboard because a ghost was coming and The Boys ran away.

A GHOST FIGHT

I saw two ghosts last night. One ghost was in a house. He kicked out the other ghost. They had a fight. One ghost ran away.

THE SKELETON PAYS A VISIT

On Friday Night we went to the pictures. When we were coming over the hill we saw a skeleton. We ran in. Our mother said to us to go to bed So we went to bed. the skeleton opened one of our windows. It had a broom with it. He saw our dog and hit him as hard as he could. Our dog was getting mad so he went in My mothers bedroom The Skeleton followed him. My Mother screamed A Policeman saw a window open so he crawled in. He saw the skeleton and he fell back through the window. He went to the Police Station and he got his helicopter He caught the skeleton and he destroyed it Then we all went back to bed again

A FRIGHT IN A FIELD

On Saturday night when I was coming home from Michaels I went over a corn field. There was a tree like a man. I ran like mad till I got home. When I got in I told my mah and went to bed. When I got into bed I saw a face looking through the window.

A STORM

We had a snow storm last Saturday and Sunday. The wind blew and it rianed very hard indeend.Then the rian changed to snow. I snowed hard and it was very fik.

I went to Scarborough. I went on some ships and I went to Filey. I went on the sands and I went in the sea and I had an ice cream and I went to Cleethorpes in a car. I went on the big wheel and I went on the roundabouts. I had a big dinner and I went to Butlins. I went on the sands. I went paddling in the sea and I had some mussels on the sands and I played ball and I had an ice cream and I went paddling in the sea and I went for tea and we went back home and I went to bed.

This is our school. It is big in school.   We write and draw about the wood and the power station and a coal mine and the river in castleford it is big we painting th wood and the coal mine and the river and the power station.

On Sunday I went to york in a car. I went fishing I caught a big fish and the fish jump up and up the fish as magers the fish like magers and I went in a cafe for dinner and I went home and on Monday I went to Scarborgh fishing I went on the rocks some people fish I took a fish home.

PAUL

paul was a apostle and one day he got struk by lighning. He was going to Damascus and to find the cristeans wehn He got strock. He dropt.

SNOW ON THE GROUND

The snow is icy and cold. One day I play at snowballs. I made a snowman in the yard. I went in for my dinner.

SNOW

Snow falls when it is cold. Snow has a lot of snowflakes. When it is warm the snow melts. It turns into water.

SPENDING A SHILLING

I have been given a shilling. I am going to buy something with it. I went to the shop for an apple. I had 9d left. I bought a orange and went home on the bus.

I went to the pictures and when I was coming home I saw a ghost appear. I ran home and I told my mother. I went to bed and the ghost appeared again. I hid under the blankets.

One night when it was my friends birthday we had tea and we played two games. Then we went outside to the shelters. We saw a ghost. We ran away.

CHASED BY A GHOST

When I got home I went to the shop. I was walking down the street when I met a ghost. I ran home and the ghost chased me to our gate. Then I went to bed.

A GHOST VISITS A CHURCH

On Monday I went to a church. A ghost saw me. I ran into the church. I saw the ghost coming in to the church I told a priest that a ghost was in his church. He got his gun and he shot the ghost but the ghost was not dead. It killed the priest. I ran to the police station. I told them what had happened. They saw the ghost. They shot at the ghost but it was not dead. It killed the policemen. Then the ghost disappeared. I ran to our house and went to bed.

THE SCREAM

One night I went to bed and a big Face came to the window. I flew under the bed. I gave a big scream. My mother cam upstairs. I was under the bed. When my mother saw me she thought I was a ghost. Then I went back to bed.

I saw a witch come in through the bedroom window. I got hold of her. She ran down the lane frightened. A car knocked her down and killed her.

Old Mother Riley went to a castle. Old Mother Riley pulled the bell. the bell rung inside the castle. An old man went to take Old Mother Riley to a room where it was dark She lit two candles. The candles went out, Old Mother Riley went down a passage way. Olf Mother Riley saw a coffin. A skeleton came out. It walked slowly down the passage way. Old Mother Riley ran fast. She jumped on a table. and on to the chandelier. She swung to the window. She went through the window. The skeleton chased Old Mother Riley. She jumped down to the field. She ran down the drive to the car. She drove away very fast.

One day I went to Ferrybrigge Power Station to see some machines. They were buzzing and throbbing all the time I went to see the fire in the machines.

The machine is in the power station I went in the power station and I saw a big machine.
The machine was clean and strong. I went to the machine it was very strong and noisy I went out and went home on the bus.

MY HOLIDAY

In the holiday I went to the mach down Wheldon Lane to see castleford versus Featherstone Rovers on Easter monday casleford won furteen five,

This residential special school was led by a dedicated headmistress with an energetic, purposeful, and "joyful" personality. There were many special occasions, much activity, and as far as was possible there was individual care and love. The resulting happiness and security is shown in some of this writing.

Girl Aged 11 years.

My Dear Joyse
I Love you Joise I will be home Friday or Thursday I hope jou are well and happy at home and Mrs sed Her Love to you and carol and Rosemaray send Them Love to you
I will pley with you and I wis kiss you with
LOVE
From
Jean
XXXXX

This child was not able to form one letter or recognize one word less than a year previous to writing this letter.

ABOUT MYSELF

On this photograph I am holding the Spanish doll which my sister brought back from Spain. There are some other dolls on the table behind me.

My doll has a yellow dress
She black hair

OUR VISIT TO A MILL

On Monday afternoon all our class went to Allison's flour mill there were 3 groups and we went all over the flour mill. there manager is called Mr. Hirst and he showed us all round the mill and after we had been round we all got a little bag of flour and the mill was very interesting in the group were Christine, Cadmon and Audrey and Gladys and Jennifer and Christine Robinsen and myself and when we went back to the little place were a girl was making some little loaves.

We went to to shop we walked ther we walked back and then we went for our dinner and then we went to play

HAVING MY HAIR PERMED

Yesterday I had my hair permed and cut Then I had some curlers and then I had some stuf on my hair and I had some waving lotion on the curles and I had my hair rinsed and I had my hair rinsed again and then I had new-traliners on the hair and I had some coutten wool over the curlers in my hair and then I had some more curlers in my hair and I sit in front of the heater to get my hair dry then Mrs. Walker tooke the curlers out of my hair.

This writing is accompanied by photographs taken whilst the operation was in process and after it was complete. There is also a piece of hair which was cut off, stuck into the script, and protected by plastic cover. This girl was greatly uplifted by this permanent wave.

Girl Aged 13.

My brother is a pest and he does not like to go to the farm and so my daddy Kicked him out of the house and shouted to him and he said i wont go to the farm, and I shall stay at homee and do some housework. I go the shop to get some things. Janet went to school and so Keith went to school together and on Satur-day I went to the shop and got some more things Sometimes on Saturday night i went to the pictures to see Elvis Presley This flim was called a Wildin the country and I saw him singing and a girl was singing with him and I think it was so nice and so good. So I said to my mother can I go to see the Billy Fary Film. It was a Once upon a dream. He was singing and I started to cry and one of my friends picked me up and said never mind Linda I said Take me home Her name was Ann West and so we did. This is the end.

Girl Aged 14.

My mother is fat She has dark curly hair. My mother is good to me. I love her very much My mother cooks the breakfast the dinner and the tea, sometimes she bakes cakes

Girl Aged 15.

THE DANCE

It was about skeletons skipping from a grave. I did not like it because I don't like seen graves.

Girl Aged 15.

In winter it snows and its cold foggy and frosty. At nights it is dark early at half past 4 before tea time. When it is dark night we stay in the house and the doors are shut and the windows are shut and the curtons are closed then the lights are on. Then in the house we play with our games like Snack's and ladder's or knit or sew or play all sorts of games. And the hedges and tree's were glittering white outside in the snow. Outside in the snow some children make a slide and through snowball's. And robin redbreast sings in the trees. Then some children go sleging down hill's and valley and on the padements in the street's. Indoor's people watched television or listen to the wireless or draw. And some people sit by the fire and read a book or knit.

Girl Aged 15.

On Friday when I went to my my Aunty I met Shandra on the bus. And I went to see Brenda. And Peter was there. and there has be a crash outside Travelas and Ruth and Kathleen and I whent bandering On Friday I went to the cleite and went I come out of the clinte I went shopping for Shandra.

Girl Aged 15.

The books I have read are about British Birds, I picked this book because I was interested in birds. And I like it very much. The second book is about what to look for in winter. I like this book too, it shows you were to look for these things and were to find them, And I think its very interesting.

Girl Aged 14.

THE DANCE

This is a silly pome and its a funny one, but its a nice pome its about a skeleton that skips about at night, now one night when everythink was still. In a churchyard ware all the graves were still out of one a skeleton came. He thought he would have a nice long dance, so he started to dance a Jolly one, and I can say if any one was walking about that night they would have been so afraid they would run away, lets get back to the skeleton. His bones did Joggle but he dont have a care to think about and at the end he was so sad that a cockerel cried morning. So the grave door opened and the skeleton had one more look and got back in his grave. I like this pome I think its a Jolly nice one.

Girl Aged 14.

On November the 5th it was bonfire night we had a very big bonfire with 18 tiers on it we had bonfire toffee and cakes, then we began to sing songs around it until it went out, On Saturday afternoon we went to the Beatles film help and I think it was fab

Girl Aged 15.

THE DANCE

I like this poem because it twlls a story and we can dance to it. I like it about the skeleton, when it says out from a grave a skeleton skips, as it twisted and turned. I wouldent like to see one come from a grave if I was walking through a graveyard.

Girl Aged 13.

MY HOLIDAY

First my Daddy came to fetch me From School and the next day We Went away for our holidays. We had to get up early and That was half past five. We had our breakfast we had for it Corn flakes and toast. and at quarter to Eight we went for the Manchester Coach and It went to Manchester We got there at quarter to Ten. Then we waited for the London Coach that got in London at Five to Six. We waited a long Time to wait for the maidstone Bus got in Maidstone just after 8 oclock we got the sutton road Bus to the top of the hill got out at The wheetshief walked up as we passed the kittchen window We saw nanny Fastening up her bags to put away we knocked on thedoor We walked in and had a cup of tea and we had some supper and Then went to Bed and next Morning my nanny gave me a cup of tea In Bed got up and went in th kitchen there was a lamp burning of oil in the kitchen, and I bought my clothese in kitchen and got dressed and afterwards I had my breakfast I had bacon and egg and potatoe. and on christmas Eve we went out for tea We had mince pies meat Pies and sesagerolls cups of tea and sandwiches and Cakes.

This poem startled the class teacher who passed it on to me as I was at the time teaching dance and drama to this remedial class in a secondary modern school.

It came about some weeks after the child had lost her mother and arose from very deep feeling and hurt and from the funeral experience.

The spelling was, I think, corrected by the teacher.

Girl Aged 13.

BLACK

A black night, all evil and cold,
Death comes about me,
Blindness touches my eyes,
I fall asleep,
And in my dreary dream I see
Funerals. Black horses carry me down to the grave.

Shadows come near me,
I can feel the EVIL going to my soul,
In a few moments I awake
And there at the foot of my bed,
My black cat stares with evil eyes.

These girls in a remedial class of a secondary modern school had great difficulty with reading and writing. For most of them, home was an uninspiring place; for many there was deprivation of a severe nature.

The class teacher, although very good and dedicated to the welfare of the girls, was unable to make up for the years of failure which these girls had already experienced, and their writing is very poor in most cases.

They express so often their longing for beauty, for happiness as they see it, and for love.

This writing is most certainly untouched by the class teacher who has helped to interpret some words.

A GOOD DAY

one day in mach [March] it was sue cakel weedday [wedding day] she was in whit satng dreen [satin dress] We ware in pan vealvt dreeand [pink velvet dresses] whit fary a raed the sthgis [white fur around the sleeves] and neke [neck] to and whit shes [shoes] and whit aclkes srst [ankle socks] we had a liveed [lovely] time in the chic [church] we were sead [sad] and Lyn and micem [myself] were carying [crying] in the chic [church] to went it was all over and we had pearh tock of sthes and cufet [confetti] over ser pepole send meak was sead to but Sue was sed allso and lueg had a walking stont [stick] to and then we went to the verge at 6 oclock we want to the maybull Home [Maypole Inn] we had feed at 10 oclock we went nome.

TREASURE

I Trea sure shep the dog if He dus not calin I cag bot coll I love He to

A GOOD DAY   WHEN I WENT TO MY COUSONS

One afternoon I went to my cousons when we go their they where all ready to go to the zoo we seen monkeys and lions when we seen the lions we went home to my cousons for tea.

TREASURE

I treasure my Braclate I would not part with it I like it most of all my other things I only where it when I go out.

sothing I would like to happen most of all
I would like to be a brisemaid for my borther and his girl-friend.

I HAVE BEN TO HABY PARK

I day I went to haby Park with my sisters and I tuken tow fonds [rounds] of Bred for the duks [ducks] we take hore [our] dinnier [dinner] we had sanwihes [sandwiches] then my mam came to We ejoury [enjoyed] it on happy Park we sore to horses go on the happy Park and my sisters went on the swings all of us went one the brig [bridge] and we walked on down the Brig and to the icecrem in the conit [cornet] my mam said gife the duks sum Bred then we went home on the Bus we enged [enjoyed] it to.

TREASURE

I treasure my Bake for a sickret [secret] I will not let heny Bodey go on my Bake went cept it for a sicret [secret] truesure [treasure].

This girl's father worked for the British Railways and so the family travelled more than would otherwise have been possible.

MY HOLDAYS

We went to Dolise [Dawlish] and on a sueday we went to Plemer [Plymouth] and we saw all the ship and all the sailors on the ship and ager [after] that we had gone spasher and tea someger and when we were going home we set maker to a sailors and then he said goodby because we were at the sasene and when we got home we had ere tea.

TREASURE

I tresasus to have a happy new year because it bing you beater look [luck].

This is the work of a 15-year-old girl with problems of maladjustment and an estimated intelligence level which would mean her inclusion in a special class or school for the slow learner.

She writes very neatly, and boldly.

WATRE MY HOME IS LIKE

My address is Thoraine Road. I live with my brother he is married to Gay. Gay is my sister in law. I live with Gay and my brother my brother's name is Ronnie, there are two navers, from upstairs, theres Mr. and Mrs. Vince and the baby.

SNEEZES!!

What is a sneeze, Well a sneeze is when you have a tigle in your noose, And you go achoo' it is corsed by peper, When you have peper on your fingers and you tuch your noose. And sometimes when you give a loud sneeze like achoo, ac choo' It makes people jump, Some people have funny sneezes, Some go aa chew', and some go Aatischoo' And some have funny sneezes still. Well people sometimes never know when they are going to sneeze, And you can even get dog sneezes and bird sneezes, birds go like choo, sneezes can come when you get a cold, animals can sneeze as well as people.

THE WEDDING BELLS

The wedding bells are ringing luvelly for the bride and brides groom. And the gestechs are waiting pashontly for the bride and bridegroom to come, And at last they come and the bridesmaids come And they get to the church and the organ -plays here comes the bride walking down the iyol Shakeing and so happy and a very pretty thing very danty, and the people smile at her, She weres a glittering cristole crown on her head and her nice long vieile and a bintyfall brides dress with all glitter on it, And the three bridesmaids follow her down the iyole, The three bridesmaids are blue with glitter on there dresses, and gold high hills on, and dimond in there head dressis.

Some schools said honestly that there was no writing which they could give to me to illustrate the quality of the children's work in this medium, and I accepted the fact that for many of these children, writing even their weekly letter home was still almost an insuperable task.

BIBLIOGRAPHY

ADAMS, D. K., *Introduction to Education: a comparative analysis*, Wordsworth Pub. Co., Belmont, California, 1966.

ADLER, A., *et al.*, *Guiding the Child*, Allen & Unwin, London, 1930.

ALDRICH, V. G., *Philosophy of Art*, Prentice-Hall, London, 1966.

ALLEN, C., *Passing School Examinations*, MacMillan, London, 1963.

ALLEN, C., *Passing Examinations*, MacMillan, London, 1963.

ALLERTON, R. and PARKER, T., *The Courage of His Convictions*, Hutchinson, London, 1962.

ALVIN, J., *Music for the Handicapped Child*, Oxford University Press, London, 1965.

ANDERSON, V., *Improving the Child's Speech*, Oxford University Press, New York, 1954.

ASHLEY, M., *Life Before Birth*, Longmans, Green, London, 1965.

AUDEN, W. H. and PEARSON, N. H. (Eds.), *Poets of the English Language*, IV, Eyre & Spottiswoode, 1952.

BANTOCK, G. H., *Education in an Industrial Society*, Faber & Faber, London, 1963.

BANTOCK, G. H. *Education and Values*, Faber & Faber, London, 1965.

BARRY, Sir Gerald, BRONOWSKI, J., FISHER, J., and HUXLEY, J., *Communication and Language*, Macdonald, 1966.

BASSETT, G. W., *Each One is Different*, Australian Council for Educational Research, arising from a conference in 1962, 1965.

BECKER, H. S., *Outsiders*, The Free Press of Glencoe, MacMillan, London, 1963.

BENTLEY, A., *Musical Ability in Children and its Measurement*, George Harrap, London, 1966.

BLACK, M., *Speech Correction in the Schools*, Prentice-Hall, London, 1964.

BLACKIE, J. *Good Enough for the Children*, Faber & Faber, London, 1963.

BLAKE, W. (Ed. Keynes, G.), *Poetry and Prose*, Nones Press, London, 1948.

BLISH, T. and MEAD, M., *Continuities in Cultural Evolution*, York University Press, 1964.

BLISHEN, E., *Roaring Boys*, Thames & Hudson, 1966.

BLOOM, B., *Stability and Change in Human Characteristics*, John Wiley, New York, London, and Sydney, 1965.

BLOOM, B., DAVIS, A., and HESS, R., *Compensatory Education for Cultural Deprivation*, Holt, Rinehart & Winston, New York, 1965.

BOLLAND, J. and SANDLER, J., *The Hampstead Psychoanalytic Index*, Monograph No. 1, International Universities Press, New York, 1966.

BORLAND, H., *High, Wide and Lonesome*, J. B. Lippincott, Philadelphia, U.S.A., 1956.

221

Bower, B., and Jeavons, P., *Infantile Spasms*, Spastic Society with Wm. Heinemann Medical Books Ltd., London, 1964.

Bowlby, J., *Child Care and the Growth of Love*, Penguin, Middlesex, 1965.

Briffault, R., *The Mothers*, Allen & Unwin, London, 1959.

Brittain, W. L. and Lowenfield, V., *Creative and Mental Growth*, MacMillan, London, 1964.

Brooks, von Wyck, *Helen Keller*, Collins, London, 1954.

Bruner, J. S., *On Knowing*, Harvard University Press, Cambridge, Mass., U.S.A., 1964.

Bruce, V., *Dance and Dance Drama in Education*, Pergamon Press, 1965.

Bruce, V. and Tooke, J. D., *An Approach to Religious Education*, Pergamon Press, 1966.

Bugelski, B. R., *The Psychology of Learning*, Methuen, London, 1959.

Burland, C. A., *Man and Art*, Studio Publications, London and New York, 1959.

Burnett, J., *Plenty and Want*, Nelson, London, 1966.

Burnett, W., *The Human Spirit*, Allen & Unwin, London, 1958.

Butler, N. R., Pringle, M. L. K., and Davie, R., 11,000 *Seven Year Olds*, Longmans, London, 1967.

Buxton, J. and Turner, M., *Gate Fever*, Cresset Press, London, 1962.

Cheshire Education Committee, *The Education of Dull Children at the Primary Stage*, University of London Press, London, 1960.

Chesser, Dr. E., *Cruelty to Children*, Gollancz, London, 1951.

Clegg, A. B., *The Excitement of Writing*, Chatto & Windus, London, 1963.

Coburn, K. (Ed.), *Inquiring Spirit (A new presentation of Coleridge)*, Routledge and Kegan Paul, 1951.

Cochrane, R. G., with Schonell, F., and McLeod, J., *The Slow Learner*, University of Queensland Press, 1962.

Cohen, L. J., *The Diversity of Meaning*, Methuen, Ltd., 1962.

Conklin, E. G., *Heredity and Environment*, Princeton University Press, 1930.

Cooper, G. and Hand, M., *Coming into their Own*, Heinemann, London, 1959.

Davis, A. and Dollard, J., *Children of Bondage*, Harper & Row, New York, 1940.

De-La-Noy, M., *Young Once Only*, Epworth Press and Methodist Publishing House, London, 1965.

Dexter, L. A., *The Tyranny of Schooling*, Basic Books Inc., New York and London, 1964.

Dodds, J. P. B., *The Slow Learner and Music*, Oxford University Press, London, 1966.

Dollard, J. and Miller, N. E., *Social Learning and Imitation*, Yale University Press, Newhaven, Conn., 1941.

Dunkel, H. B., *Whitehead on Education*, Ohio State University Press, Ohio, 1965.

Dushkin and Frankenstein, *Studies in Education, John Dewey School of Education*, Magnes Press, Hebrew University, Jerusalem, 1963.

DYBWARD, G., *Challenges in Mental Retardation*, Columbia University Press, New York, 1964.

EARL, C. J. C., *Subnormal Personalities*, Baillière, Tindall & Cox, London, 1961.
EDMUNDS, F., *Rudolf Steiner Education*, Rudolf Steiner Press, 1962.

FEATHERSTONE, W. B., *Teaching the Slow Learner*, Bureau of Publications, Teachers College, Columbia University, New York, 1951.
FELKIN, F. W., *Letters to Schoolmasters*, Sheldon Press, London, 1931.
FINK, A., *Games of Crime*, Pennsylvania State University Press, Pa., 1962.
FROMM, E., *The Forgotten Language*, Gollancz, London, 1952.
FRYE, N., *The Educated Imagination*, Indiana University Press, Bloomington, 1964.

GABO, N., *Of Divers Arts*, Faber & Faber, London, 1962.
GARDNER, K., *Towards Literacy*, Blackwell & Mott, Oxford, 1965.
GENTER, L., *Adventure in Curative Education*, New Knowledge Books, East Grinstead, 1962.
GESELL, A., *Infant and Child in the Culture of Today*, Hamish Hamilton, London, 1943.
GIBBERD, K., *About Your Schools*, Macdonald & Co., London, 1965.
GIKBY, R. G. and HUTT, M. L., *The Mentally Retarded Child*, Allyn & Bacon, Boston, 1959.
GLUCK, S. and E., *Delinquency in the Making*, Harper, New York, 1952.
GOODACRE, E. J., *Reading in Infant Classes*, National Foundation for Educational Research in England and Wales, 1967.
GOODLAD, J. (Ed.), *65th Year Book of the National Society for the Study of Education*, Part II, University of Chicago Press, 1963.
GOSLING, R., *Sam Talal*, Faber & Faber, London, 1962.
GRAHAM, M., *Human Needs*, Cresset Press, London, 1951.
GRAY, W. S., *The Teaching of Reading and Writing*, U.N.E.S.C.O., 1963.
GRÖZINGER, W., *Scribbling, Drawing and Painting*, Faber & Faber, London, 1966.
GRUNZBURG, H. C., *Social Rehabilitation of the Subnormal*, Baillière, Tindall & Cox, London, 1960.
GULLIFORD, R. and TANSLEY, A., *The Education of Slow Learning Children*, Routledge and Kegan Paul, London, 1960.

HARGREAVES, D. H., *Social Relations in a Secondary School*, Routledge and Kegan Paul, London, 1967.
HARRIS, I. D. and M. D., *Emotional Blocks to Learning*, The Free Press of Glencoe, U.S.A., 1961.
HERMAN, K., *Reading Disability*, Thomas, Springfield, Illinois, 1959.
HERMELIN, B. and O'CONNER, N., *Speech and Thought in Severe Subnormality*, Pergamon Press, Oxford, 1963.
HIGHFIELD, M. E., *The Young School Failure*, Oliver & Boyd, Edinburgh, 1949.
HILDEBRAND, J. H., *Is Intelligence Important?*, Macmillan, New York, 1963.
HILLIARD, L. T. and KIRMAN, B. H., *Mental Deficiency*, Churchill, London, 1957.
HIMELSTEIN, P., *Readings on the Exceptional Child*, Methuen, London, 1962.

HOLBROOK, D., *English for the Rejected*, Cambridge University Press, 1964.
HOLBROOK, D., *The Secret Places*, Methuen, London, 1964.
HOLBROOK, D., *The Quest for Love*, Methuen, London, 1964.
HOLMES, E., *What is and Might be*, Constable, London, 1912.
HOLT, J., *How Children Fail*, Pitman, New York, 1964.
HOLT, K. S., *Assessment of Cerebral Palsy*, Lloyd-Luke, London, 1965.
HOOD, R., *Homeless Borstal Boys*, Bell, London, 1966.
HORST and RUSSELL, *Modern Dance Forms*, Impulse Publications, San Francisco, 1963.
HOURD, M., *The Education of the Poetic Spirit*, New Education Book Club, 1949.
HOWE, E. G., *Cure or Heal*, Allen & Unwin, London, 1965.
HUDSON, L., *Contrary Imaginations*, Methuen, London, 1966.
HUGHES, T., *Here Today*, Hutchinson, London, 1966.

ILLINGWORTH, R. S., *The Normal School Child*, Heinemann, London, 1964.

JACKSON, B., *Streaming: an education system*, Institute of Community Studies, Routledge and Kegan Paul, London, 1964.
JASPER, K., *The Nature of Psychotherapy*, Manchester University Press, 1962.
JEFFREYS, M. C. V., *Mystery of Man*, Pitman, London, 1957.
JEPHCOTT, P., *A Troubled Area*, Faber & Faber, London, 1965.
JESPERSON, O., *Mankind, Nation and Individual*, Allen & Unwin, London, 1946.
JORDAN, D., *Childhood and Movement*, Blackwell & Mott, London, 1966.

KAHN, J. and NURSTEN, J., *Unwillingly to School*, Pergamon Press, Oxford, 1964.
KAPER, N., *The New Landscape*, Paul Theobald, Chicago.
KAUFMAN, I., *Art and Education in Contemporary Culture*, MacMillan, New York, 1966.
KEPES, G., *New Landscape in Art and Science*, Paul Theobald, Chicago, 1956.
KEPES, G. (Ed.), *The Nature and Art of Motion*, Studio Vista, London, 1965.
KEPHANT, N. C., *The Slow Learner in the Classroom*, Charles E. Merrill Books, Inc., Columbus, Ohio, 1960.
KERSHAW, J. D., *Handicapped Children*, Heinemann Medical Books Ltd., 1961.
KOESTLER, A., *The Act of Creation*, Hutchinson, 1964.
KRISHNAMURTI, J., *Education and the Significance of Life*, Gollancz, London, 1955.
KRISHNAMURTI, J., *The First and Last Freedom*, Gollancz, London, 1954.
KRISHNAMURTI, J., *Life Ahead*, Gollancz, London, 1963.
KUETHE, J. and WALTON, J. (Ed.), *The Discipline of Education*, University of Wisconsin Press, Madison, 1963.

LACK, A., *The Teaching of Language to Deaf Children*, Oxford University Press, London, 1955.
LAEWY, H., *More about the Backward Child*, Staples Press, London, 1957.
LARRABEE, E. and MEYERSOHN, R. (Ed.), *Mass Leisure*, Glencoe Free Press, Illinois, 1961.
LASSELL, M., *Wellington Road*, Routledge and Kegan Paul, London, 1962.
LEVINSON, A., *The Mentally Retarded Child*, Allen & Unwin, London, 1955.

LEWIS, H., *Deprived Children*, Oxford University Press, London, 1954.

LIEBMAN, S. (Ed.), *The Emotional Problems of Childhood*, J. B. Lippincott Co., U.S.A., 1958.

LINDSAY, Z., *Art for Spastics*, Mills & Boon, London, 1966.

LISITZLEY, G., *Four Ways of Being Human*, Viking, New York, 1956.

LOWENSTEIN, O., *The Senses*, Pelican, 1966.

LURIA, A. R. and YUDOVIC, I. I., *Speech and Development of Mental Processes in the Child*, Staples Press, London, 1959.

MACKENZIE, R. F., *Escape from the Classroom*, Collins, 1965.

MCGLASHAN, A., *The Savage and Beautiful Country*, Chatto & Windus, London, 1966.

MCKENZIE, J. G., *Guilt*, Allen & Unwin, London, 1962.

MARITAIN, J., *The Degrees of Knowledge: a new translation*, Geoffrey Bles, London, 1959.

MASON, S. E. (Ed.), *Signs, Signals and Symbols*, Methuen, London, 1963.

MATHER, K., *Human Diversity*, Oliver & Boyd, Edinburgh, 1964.

MAYS, J. BARRON, *On the Threshold of Delinquency*, Liverpool University Press, 1959.

MAYS, J. BARRON, *The School in its Social Setting*, Longmans, 1967.

MEARNS, H., *The Education of Youth in the Creative Arts*, Constable, London, 1958.

MENDAY, R. P. and WILES, J., *The Everlasting Childhood*, Gollancz, London, 1959.

MERBAUM, M. and SOUTHWELL, E. (Ed.), *Personality Readings in Theory and Research*, Wadsworth Publishing Co., California, 1965.

MEREDITH, P., *Instruments of Communication*, Pergamon Press, Oxford, 1966.

MERSKEY, H., *Psychiatric Illness*, Baillière, Tindall & Cox, London, 1963.

MEYERS, C. R., *Measurement in Physical Education*, Ronald Press Co., New York, 1962.

MILLER, D., *Growth to Freedom*, Tavistock Publications Ltd., London, 1964.

MONEY, J. (Ed.), *Reading Disability*, Baltimore, 1962.

MORSE, M., *The Unattached*, Pelican, 1965.

MURPHY, BARCLAY, *et al.*, *The Widening World of Childhood*, Basic Books Inc., New York, 1962.

MYKLEBUST, H. R., *Development and Disorder of Written Language*, vol. 1, Grune & Stratten, New York and London, 1966.

NEEDHAM, J. (Ed.), *Teachers of Nations*, Cambridge University Press, 1942.

OSBORNE, E., *The Family Scrapbook*, World's Work (1913) Ltd., Surrey, 1953.

PARK, J., *Bertrand Russell on Education*, Allen & Unwin, London, 1964.

PATON, A., *Cry, The Beloved Country*, J. Cape, London, 1948.

PEEL, E. A., *The Pupil's Thinking*, Oldbourne, London, 1966.

PELONE, A. J., *Helping the Visually Handicapped Child in a Regular Class*, Teachers College, Columbia University, U.S.A., 1957.

PETERS, R. S. (Ed.), *The Concept of Education*, Routledge and Kegan Paul, 1967.

PETRIE, M., *Art and Regeneration*, Paul Elek, London, 1946.

PHILIP, A. E., *Family Failure*, Faber & Faber, London, 1963.

PHILIPS, M., *The Education of the Emotions*, Allen & Unwin, London, 1937.

PIAGET, J., *The Construction of Reality in the Child*, Basic Books Inc., New York, 1959.

PIAGET, J., *The Language and Thought of the Child*, Routledge and Kegan Paul, London, 1948.

PICKARD, P. M., *The Activity of Children*, Longmans, London, 1965.

PIETZNER, C. (Ed.), *Aspects of Curative Education*, Aberdeen University Press for the Camphill Movement, 1966.

PLAYFAIR, G. and SINGTON, D., *Crime, Punishment and Cure*, Secker & Warburg, London, 1965.

PRESTON, D. V., *A Handbook for Modern Educational Dance*, Macdonald & Evans, 1963.

PRINGLE, M. I. K., *Deprivation and Education*, Longmans, London, 1965.

RAMSEY, I. (Ed.), *Biology and Personality*, Blackwell & Mott, Oxford, 1965.

RANKIN, H. D., *Plato and the Individual*, Methuen, 1964.

RAYNAL, M., *Modern Painters*, vol. 3.

REEVES, J. (Edited and introduced), *The Cassell Book of English Poetry*, Cassell, London, 1965.

RIESE, H., *Heal the Hurt Child*, University of Chicago Press, Chicago and London, 1962.

RIESSMANN, F., *The Culturally Deprived Child*, Harper & Bros., New York and London, 1962.

ROAB, E. and SELZNICK, G., *Major Social Problems*, Rew Peterson, Illinois, 1959.

ROBERTSON, S. M., *Rosegarden and Labyrinth: a study in art education*, Routledge and Kegan Paul, London, 1963.

ROBINS, L. M., *Deviant Children Grow Up*, Livingston, Edinburgh, 1966.

ROSEN, E., *Dance in Psychotherapy*, Bureau of Publications, Teachers College, Columbia University, New York, 1957.

ROWE, E., *Failure in School: aspects of the problem in Hong Kong*, University of Hong Kong, 1966.

RUBENFELD, S., *Family of Outcasts*, Collier, MacMillan, London, 1965.

RUGG, H., *Imagination*, Harper & Row, New York, 1963.

RUSKIN, J., *Modern Painter*, vol. 3, Smith, Elder & Co., London, 1843.

RUSSELL, J., *Creative Dance in the Primary School*, MacDonald & Evans, 1965.

SADLER, J. E., *J. A. Comenius and the Concept of Universal Education*, Allen & Unwin, London, 1966.

SAPORTA, S. (Ed.), *Psycholinguistics*, Holt, Rinehart & Winston, New York, 1961.

SEGAL, S. S., *11 + Rejects*, Schoolmaster Publishing Co. Ltd., London, 1961.

SEGAL, S. S., *No Child is Ineducable*, Pergamon Press, Oxford, 1967.

SESONAKE, A., *What is Art?*, Oxford University Press, London, 1965.

SHEED, F. J., *Society and Sanity*, Sheed & Ward, New York, 1953.

SPINDLER, G. P., *Education and Culture*, Holt, Rinehart & Winston, New York, 1955.

STEINER, R., *The Kingdom of Childhood*, Rudolf Steiner Press, London, 1964.

STODDARD, G. D., *Frontiers in Education*, Stanford University Press, 1945.

STODDARD, G. D., *The Meaning of Intelligence*, MacMillan, New York, 1949.

STOTT, D. H., *Delinquency and Human Nature*, Carnegie United Kingdom Trust, Comely Park House, Dunfermline, Fife, 1950.

SUTTLE, J. D., *Origins of Love and Hate*, Penguin, Middlesex, 1945.

TANSLEY, A., *Reading and Remedial Reading*, Routledge and Kegan Paul, London, 1967.

THACKERAY, R. M., *Creative Music in Education*, Novello, London, 1965.

TODD (Ed.), *The Arts, Artists and Thinkers: an enquiry into the place of the arts in human life*, Longmans, London, 1958.

TOURNIER, P., *The Strong and the Weak*, S.C.M. Press, London, 1963.

TRAPP, P., *Readings on the Exceptional Child*, Methuen, London, 1962.

TRICKER, R. and B., *The Science of Movement*, Mills & Bon, London, 1967.

TUCKER, J., *Honourable Estates*, Gollancz, London, 1966.

VALENTINE, C. W., *The Experimental Psychology of Beauty*, Methuen, London, 1962.

VAZ, E. W., *Middle-class Juvenile Delinquency*, Harper & Row, 1967.

VIOLA, W., *Child Art*, University of London Press, 1944.

VYGOTSKY, L. S., *Thought and Language*, M. & T. Press, Massachusetts Institute of Technology, 1962.

WALSH, W. (Ed.), *The Use of Imagination*, Chatto & Windus, London, 1959.

WATSON, J. A. F., *The Child and the Magistrate*, Jonathan Cape, London, 1965.

WATTS, A. F., *The Language and Mental Development of Children*, George Harrap, London, 1948.

WEST, D. J., *The Young Offender*, Penguin, Middlesex, 1967.

WILBUR, R., *The New Landscape*, Paul Theobald, Chicago.

WILLS, D., *Throw Away Thy Rod*, Gollancz, London, 1960.

WILSON, H., *Delinquency and Child Neglect*, Allen & Unwin, London, 1962.

WINNICOTT, D. W., *The Child and the Outside World*, Tavistock Publications, London, 1957.

WISE, A., *Communications in Speech*, Longmans, London, 1965.

WISEMAN, *Education and Environment*, Manchester University Press, 1964.

YGTESIAS, J. R. C., *Education for Living*, Cory Adams & Mackay, Stirling, 1965.

YOUNG, M., *Innovation and Research in Education*, Institute of Community Studies, Routledge and Kegan Paul, London, 1965.

ZIEGFELD, E., *Education and Art*, U.N.E.S.C.O., 1953.

ZWEIG, F., *The Quest for Fellowship*, Heinemann, London, 1965.

Articles, Pamphlets, and Reports

The Socio-economic distribution of families having children admitted to Craven Lodge Residential School, Melton Mowbray, Leicestershire, April 1952 to December 1961.

A. D. B. CLARKE and A. M. CLARKE, How constant is the I.Q.? *Lancet*, vol. 2, p. 877, 1953.

Ten Years of Change, West Riding Education Committee, 1953.

Education 1954–64, West Riding Education Committee, 1964.

J. DOBBS, M.Ed. thesis, Durham, The influence of music on the retarded child, 1954.

The handicapped child, *The Practitioner*, vol. 174, 1955.

M. D. SHERIDAN, The intelligence of 100 neglected mothers, *Medical Journal*, vol. 1, p. 91, 1956.

Sensory Deprivation: A Symposium held at Harvard Medical School, Harvard University Press, 1961.

Youth Employment, vol. 14, no. 2, winter, 1961–62.

Forward Trends (Ed. S. Segal), International Conference, the Guild of Teachers of Backward Children, 1962.

Half our Future, Newsom Committee, H.M.S.O., 1962.

A Second Survey of Books for Backward Readers, University of Bristol Institute of Education, University of London Press, 1962.

J. N. OLIVER, Ph.D. thesis, The interrelations between the various growth characteristics of educationally subnormal boys in residential schools, University of Birmingham, 1962–63.

The Health of the School Child, H.M.S.O., 1962 and 1963.

F. D. PARKER, The physical education of educationally subnormal children, offprint from *Public Health*, January 1963.

P. MEREDITH, Mind and Movement, Eastbourne, September 1963.

G. GINNEVER, Learning to Live, Leicester College of Education Lecture, 1963.

Report of the Conference Music for the Handicapped Child, Wye College, Kent, April 1963.

The Arts in Education: Studies in Education, University of London Institute of Education, 1963.

Fine Arts: Education in the Soviet Union, U.S. Dept. of Health, Education, and Welfare, 1963.

Progress Report on the Special Unit at St. Francis Residential School, Birmingham, City of Birmingham Education Committee, January 1963 to June 1964.

Evidence to the Plowden Committee given by S. Segal, Chairman, The Guild of Teachers of Backward Children, published by the National Society for Mentally Handicapped Children, 1964.

Education for teaching, *Journal of the Association of Teachers in Colleges and Departments of Education*, 1964.

Language Development and Speech, the Dame Ellen Pinsent School, Birmingham, 1964.

Planning the Curriculum, the Dame Ellen Pinsent School, Birmingham, 1964.

Children with Communication Problems, Proceedings of a conference called by the Invalid Children's Aid Association, London, 7 April 1964.

Criteria of Success in English, National Association for the Teaching of English, 1965.

Research Papers in Physical Education, Carnegie College of Physical Education, June 1965.

Non-streaming in the Junior School, Forum, P.S.W. (Educational) Publications, Leicester, 1966.

Multiple Marking of English Compositions, H.M.S.O., 1966.

Physical Education Association of Great Britain and Ireland—Reports, 1966.
P. BIRD, Prayer and creative art, *Quarterly Review of the Community of the Resurrection*, Michaelmas, 1966.
S. M. MAXWELL (Ed.), *Emotionally Disturbed Children*, Proceedings of the Annual Study Conference, Association of Workers for Maladjusted Children, Pergamon Press, 1966.
Children and their Primary Schools, The Central Advisory Council for Education (the Plowden Report), H.M.S.O., 1967.

INDEX